GREETINGS FROM WISDOM, MONTANA

Other Books by Ruth Rudner

Wandering: A Walker's Guide to the Mountain Trails
    of Europe
Huts and Hikes in the Dolomites
Off and Walking
Forgotten Pleasures
Bitterroot to Beartooth: Hiking Southwest Montana

GREETINGS
from
WISDOM,
MONTANA

Ruth Rudner

FULCRUM, INC.
Golden, Colorado

Library of Congress Cataloging-in-Publication Data

Rudner, Ruth.
    Greetings from Wisdom, Montana / Ruth Rudner.
        p. cm.
    ISBN 1-55591-045-9
    1. Wisdom Region (Mont.)—Description and travel—1981-
2. Rudner, Ruth—Homes and haunts—Montana—Wisdom
    Region.
    I. Title.
    F739.W57R833 1989
    978.6'69–dc20   89-33077
                                                           CIP

Printed in the United States of America
10 9 8 7 6 5 4 3 2 1

Fulcrum, Inc.
Golden, Colorado

78340◄

For Jim Goldsmith

to whom this one was always promised

Contents

Not long after I arrived in Montana the first summer I lived here, I was driving from Big Sky to Anaconda to attend a meeting of the Senate Public Lands Subcommittee, convened to hear arguments for and against new wilderness designations in the state. On the way I passed two road signs. One pointed to Opportunity, the other to Wisdom. I was relieved to be going to Anaconda, because I wasn't sure which of the other routes I would pick. Then I decided that the roads we travel must be by chance, because any choosing leaves something out, and only chance allows all things in.

August 1985

In Chief Joseph's Lodge

Nothing covers the lodgepoles anymore. Rising in a circle on the ground, they lean toward one another to the point where they are lashed together, then spread beyond that to form a cup open to the sky. Ceasing to be the framework for a tipi, they become, instead, the entire structure. A tipi skeleton. An abstract tipi, a form, a sculpture, a memory. The tipis are open to a sun that burns hot, white, relentlessly on the Big Hole Valley. The valley's grass is yellow by midsummer, and without shadows.

The Nez Percé camped here for a few days in August 1877. They pastured two thousand horses on the hill across the Big Hole River from this camp where the tipis stand. Beyond the camp the river flows dark, its edges defined by the willows. The sage-covered hill on the far side of the river is bare of trees in the center, but thickly treed to the north where the siege took place, and to the south, where a nineteen-hundred-pound howitzer was placed. From the Big Hole Battlefield Visitor Center on a high bluff above the Indian camp, you look down on the camp and the river and across to the hillside, although you cannot see the howitzer. Rather, you cannot see the howitzer replacement—the original is now a display inside the Visitor Center. Nor can you see it from anywhere below it on either side of the river, so well is it hidden by trees. The range of the original cannon was one thousand feet. It was placed one thousand two hundred feet from the camp.

From the Visitor Center the hillside seems just another Montana view, dusty green where the sage is, black-green in the trees sloping down to the silver-green of the willows. The greens of the hill evolve into the yellow-gold of the flats. The colors are subtle, but they form Montana. Color, space and line form Montana: the line of the river, the trees, the hillside against the sky, the long stretch of grass up and down the valley.

Heat molds the summer. This summer is even hotter than usual, and tinder-dry. There is little to stop the forest fires that are raging throughout the state.

Smoke veils the clear Montana sky, covering the distant mountains with a haze they do not own. Campfires have been forbidden. People have been asked not to cut down trees with chain saws because of the danger a spark might ignite yet another fire. If you leave the shadow of forest, you walk enveloped in heat and thirst, as if your thirst comes from outside you, then wraps you in it, while the sun burns into you in a way that nothing stops. The dust of the earth powders up about your ankles and settles on your clothes and shoes. The light stays even and hot and enters your mind before it reaches your eyes.

The Visitor Center is efficiently utilitarian, as most structures erected by the U.S. Departments of the Interior or Agriculture seem to be, fulfilling some latent longing for efficiency the government has no other means to implement. Or perhaps the government has so instinctive a longing for the military that it is forever constructing barracks. Certainly there is no instinct to erect buildings that belong to the landscape in which they are built, or to the traditions of that landscape. This is perhaps not serious, except this particular building (which *does* possess an architectural furbelow more or less shaped like a tipi) serves as a monument to honored ground, a particular piece of land the United States Army happened to have lost. Temporarily, to be sure, but lost nonetheless. Temporarily, because the Nez Percé could not stay to hold the land. Knowing more soldiers would come, racing time and government troops in their attempt to reach Canada for what they believed would be a chance to live in pride and the honor of their history, they had to leave. What do we commemorate by erecting one of "our" buildings to mark one of "their" victories, besides our ability to make victory or defeat in battle largely a verbal exercise?

No one walks along the dusty road into the Nez Percé camp but my friend and I. Before we reach the first of the tipis, we come upon the first monuments to the fallen. Blue hats made of wood and perched on sticks mark where soldiers fell; tan hats mark the civilian volunteers. The fallen Indians are marked by wooden white feathers. The feathers cover almost the entire stick so that the markers for the Indians look less like popsicles than do those for the white men. Perhaps the popsicle is as suitable a monument to the white man as anyone has devised. The popsicle and the spaceship.

Across the river, on the hillside where the siege took place, the U.S. Government has placed a six-ton Vermont granite monument, like a giant tombstone, to the fallen soldiers. The names of the soldiers who died are cut into the back.

The monument to the Indians is the camp, the empty tipis, the hot sun and silent grass, the river flowing—low this year, but flowing, as if no one had died in it or ever hidden in its willows.

There is a trail guide to the village. A thin blue pamphlet called *Nez Percé Camp* and published by the National Park Service is available for twenty-five cents from a wooden box near the dusty road. Honor system. If you prefer not to buy one, you may use it and return it to the box after your tour of the camp. Little wooden numbered signs on the ground correspond to the numbers in the booklet so that it is possible to stop every few feet and read a succinct account of which chief lived in the tipi in front of you, who fought on this spot, who died here, who did not die. You walk along and read about these things and the sun burns into you as it must have in August 1877, except that then the hides covering the tipis offered shelter from its rays. There is a coolness along the river. The coolness was there then, too.

Natalekin, an old man, was the first Indian killed. His eyesight poor, he saw nothing amiss as he rode his horse across the river to check on the herd. He rode directly into the gunfire of three civilian volunteers.

The volunteers, never known for their discipline, got the fighting started before the army was quite ready. There were about 125 warriors among the 800 Nez Percé; of the 63 to 90 Nez Percé who died, 30 were warriors. Of 132 soldiers, 20 died. A number of volunteers also died, and some ran away.

Chief Joseph did not die. He was not the only chief, but as a wise man and counselor, he has become for us symbolic leader of the entire tribe. In the sorrow of his words he feeds us poetry that assuages our white souls. We accept more easily the defeat of those we conquer if they provide us eloquence. "Hear me, my chiefs, I am tired; my heart is sick and sad. From where the sun now stands, I will fight no more forever." We are somehow less guilty in the presence of kings.

My friend and I walk slowly the length of the village. At the bend in the trail, which is near the bend in the river, the north end of the camp stands as a denser jumble of tipis than this southern end where the tipis of the chiefs stand. Chief Joseph's tipi is near the river, after the bend. We come to his tipi, and I enter it. I ask my friend to come inside.

"No," he says, "I have not been invited."

But I believe I am invited by the homage I pay. I come

in homage to his wisdom, to his longing for a place to live in peace, to his soul, his language, his people, his birthright to America. I come asking his spirit to embrace me. I come to embrace his spirit and the soul of this place. I understand it as a place to rest on the search for a place to live.

There was hope along this river. The water and the willows offered coolness. This was forage for the horses and food for the people. The valley offered respite, offered time. Now there is only time here, and the river and that spirit we needed to break. I stand in this lodge to give the spirit back, to ask forgiveness of it. Is this lodge not a holy place?

When I die, could any friend do more for my soul than come and stand in my house, to stand inside what I had made, to ask to be embraced by my spirit? I have not overstepped my bounds. I was invited.

Later I go to the river and put my hands in it. The water runs over my palms, my wrists. It is not the same water because the fact of a river is that the water is always new, but it is the same river, dark and cool with willows on its banks and fish in its depths. It flows through the Big Hole in this hot summer and does not pretend to offer peace. Yet, in the hot silence of the afternoon, it offers respite, a moment so natural that it almost seems possible to believe we will be allowed a place to live.

Building a Fence

It was snowing when I arrived in Montana the twelfth of June. My father's birthday. I had never spent his birthday in a snowstorm before. My father, on the other hand, was observing it at home in Florida, where the temperature was in the eighties. America is a big country.

I moved into the studio condominium I had rented for two hundred dollars a month at the base of the Big Sky ski area, making it as much mine as possible by throwing Mexican blankets over most things, placing straw baskets in strategic spots and calling the rental agency to come take away an enormous and quite dreadful red-and-gold oil painting of a cowboy on a horse. About six feet high and four feet wide, it took up a good part of the room. They also took the television set I didn't want, but when I moved out a few months later they forgot they had it and asked—with a certain amount of tact, it's true—what I might have done with it.

I knew no one in Montana. Choosing my particular condominium as a place to live was more or less guaranteed to keep me from meeting anyone. Nine winding miles up the mountain road from the valley, six miles up from the Meadow Village where all the summer activity takes place, and forty long, twisting canyon miles from Bozeman, there was not a lot happening up there. I hadn't considered that when I rented it sight unseen, because it was cheap and because I liked the idea of being on the mountain. From the picture window, which was also the only window—it faced the parking lot and beyond that, Lone Mountain—I could watch dawn arrive and day end over the mountain.

Lone Mountain becomes an obsession with anyone who watches it for long. People take on a personal relationship with it, referring to it as "my mountain." They are always a bit taken aback when someone else refers to it as "my mountain," as if that were not possible, as if they stood in unique relation to it. Like one's dog or one's lover, Lone Mountain is an intense possession.

BUILDING A FENCE

* *

After a few days I drove down the twisting road to the rental agency in the canyon and met the landlord. He had black, wiry hair, a black moustache, perfectly fitting jeans and expensive cowboy boots. He looked like an ad for Montana, some ultimate combination of an Italian actor and a cowboy. In fact, he was an ex-cop from Chicago who had lived here about twelve years. As a real estate broker in Montana he was shot at less often than as a cop in Chicago, although the game seemed more or less the same—cops and robbers or cowboys and Indians—some variation of growing up macho in America.

He asked if I would like to help him build a fence on Saturday. "I don't know how to build a fence," I answered, thinking at the same time that this would be a wonderful opportunity to learn; that if I intended to stay in Montana, knowing how to build a fence could be a useful thing. Maybe even get me a job. I hoped he would offer to show me.

"You don't need to know anything," he said.

The real estate office was a low building surrounded by fields that back up to the edge of the Gallatin Range. The family horses grazed in a large field to the south, at that time enclosed by a wire fence. The landlord wanted a wooden fence in its place, all wood for the corral at the back of the building and wood posts that would be connected by wire for the big field.

"Then I'd like to," I said.

"Eight o'clock Saturday morning," he said. "Buy you breakfast. All my friends will be here."

How clever this had been of me, I thought. I would learn a trade and meet some people. Maybe this would become my world, my entrée into Montana. A builder of fences. Perhaps if I concentrated on fences long enough I would become a poet, something there is that builds a fence.

The landlord was already there when I arrived at the office on Saturday morning. A few minutes later four men drove up, each in a separate, large and expensive four-by-four. We took two of the vehicles a few miles down Route 191 to the Corral Bar and Cafe. Route 191 winds its way through the narrow Gallatin Canyon ninety-seven miles from Bozeman to Yellowstone National Park. As the main truck route between Bozeman and West Yellowstone, the big eighteen-wheelers fly down it like it was Interstate 80. Tourists, on the other hand, dawdle, sometimes stopping dead in the middle of the road to watch a herd of bighorn sheep or mule deer, or a moose, coyote, bear, eagle or marmot. Usually they stop dead on the far side of a curve. This is not the safest road in America.

We occupied a long table in the center of the cafe. The men all seemed to be from Idaho. One of them, apparently rich, owned a large house on the Gallatin River across the road from the cafe, in addition to whatever it was he had in Idaho. Another owned a chain of restaurants in the West, but came originally from Queens. He wore a cowboy hat. Two former cowboys had obviously done well in something other than cowboying, although what was not clear. All the men, including the landlord, wore leather belts with flowers and swirls and their own names hand-tooled into them. These had been made by one of the former cowboys. The two were brothers, or perhaps one of them was the brother of the rich man. In any case, there were some brothers present. The Chinese would probably say you couldn't tell any of them apart.

None of the men had much to say to me. I couldn't think of anything to say to them either. I wished we could finish breakfast quickly and get to work. Whatever building a fence consisted of, it probably didn't require a lot of conversation.

A few more men had arrived by the time we returned to the office, adding some ordinary pickup trucks to the assortment of fancy four-by-fours in the parking area. We began at once, pulling off the old fence wire and getting rid of the old metal stakes. After measuring the post intervals, we laid the new posts where they would be needed. The posts were large and heavy, and dragging them into place was hard work. It was probably harder work for me than for the men, but they hauled more posts at a time, so maybe it evened out. This done, the post holes could be dug.

The actual digging was done by a hole-making machine operated by the tractor to which it was attached. It lifted a thick and pointed rod, then rammed it into the earth. Sometimes we had to remove rocks from the hole site. Whole families of field mice, tiny, gray things, lay suddenly exposed, dazed by the light. It always took them a few moments before they seemed to realize they should run. Then they scattered quickly.

The cool June day grew warm. At lunchtime the landlord's secretary appeared with sandwiches, soft drinks and beer, all of it eagerly consumed on the tailgates of the pickups. Later on in my stay in Montana, I was often to eat on the tailgate of a pickup, sometimes as a celebration after a backpacking trip, complete with wine that had been left in the truck; other times it was the food planned for a trek that just didn't start because the weather was so bad. Then the truck became dining room, sleeping quarters and reading room. This sometimes went on for days.

By late afternoon most of the men had left. The landlord, the rich man and I continued making the post holes so that all the posts could be placed on Sunday. We worked until after six, when the landlord, asking if I would join them for dinner, announced they would pick me up in an hour. Driving back to the condo, I wondered at my accepting. It had seemed somehow disloyal not to, although I felt it would have been better, more dignified, perhaps, not to have accepted. It would have been good to appear independent, as if it had been only fence building that interested me.

We drove into Bozeman in the rich man's big four-wheel-drive. Obviously pleased at the power of his vehicle, he drove fast except when his radar detector indicated a police car somewhere nearby. He himself was large and powerful and exuded an aura of perfect control, a sense he would not crash. We joined the others at a restaurant the locals consider the best in town. To me it looks like any motel restaurant, with food of no particular distinction. Maybe when I've been here longer I'll appreciate this more.

I sat next to the landlord, who was friendly and attentive, but I felt extraneous. We were a large party, having accumulated various women before the cocktail hour. After dinner we drove back up the canyon to Stacey's Bar in Gallatin Gateway. Stacey's is the local cowboy bar, the macho hangout, the focal point of the

Canyon action, coarse and raw and raucous enough to suit the proper western taste. Nobody asked me to dance. I seem to have been the only woman in the bar nobody asked to dance. I felt embarrassed for the landlord, who had been responsible for bringing me here and could now see that I was not interesting to anyone. Even he did not ask me to dance.

In the morning only the landlord, the rich man and I turned up to work. The landlord and I hoisted the posts into the holes and held them, while the rich man drove the tractor that pounded them in. It was necessary to align the pounding mechanism with the post in an exact way or the post went in crooked. It was also necessary to judge with one's eye whether the posts were pounded in to the same height. Several times the landlord miscalculated the placing of a post, and the rich man scolded him, impatient, the way a close friend is, a close friend or a husband. They were tired and probably hung over; the day was a gray one and the work hard. Eventually a couple of other men turned up, but stayed only a short time. I worked until about seven o'clock, wanting to leave earlier but feeling too awkward to leave. I felt I somehow had a duty to them; that, having said I wanted to build a fence, it would have been wrong to leave before the fence was finished. I guess I felt a duty to myself too. I had set out to build a fence, and I intended to see it built. I think that's how I had felt about the dinner as well—that it was part of building the fence and had to be seen through. But finally I wanted out. I said I had some plans.

All the posts had to be in before morning when the machine was to be returned. The two of them, the landlord and the rich man, continued working late into the night. When I drove by the next day all the posts were in, but nothing more was done on the fence for several months.

Fourth of July

I began waiting for Bruce at three in the afternoon, although he could not possibly arrive before ten. He said he would bring meat from a bear he had shot the previous fall.

It was almost a month that I had been in Montana. Until the preceding February, my not wholly irrational terror of grizzly bears had kept me out of Montana the first forty years of my life. In February, an assignment to write a ski story brought me out while the bears were hibernating. When I deplaned in Kalispell then, I had a sense of coming home, one of those experiences people occasionally have in places they have never been that seem so reassuring a proof of reincarnation. I stayed only ten days. Now I had returned with a commission to write a book about the mountains of southwestern Montana.

There are fewer bears in southwestern Montana than there are up north, around Kalispell and Glacier National Park; but black bears are everywhere in the region, and grizzlies live in the areas abutting Yellowstone, as well as in the park. My fear was no less than ever, but because I wanted to do the book, I believed myself less vulnerable to bear attack. The operating theory is that if you do something just for the pleasure of it, you endanger yourself, but if the same thing is in the line of work, ordinarily inaccessible reserves of daring appear that make you invulnerable. This may be an overly puritanical outlook on life, but if it works, I think it should be used. Where there is a job to be done, one usually lives through it, sometimes even well.

Bruce was the first person I had invited to my house. It had been a year since I had expected a man for dinner, a year since my husband had stopped coming home for dinner. Or at all. Excited about the prospect of preparing dinner for a man, I had already made the salad, peeled asparagus, washed mushrooms and spent considerable time trying to decide whether or not to put candles on the table. This occasion was not a romantic one but just the beginning of a backpacking weekend. Dinner was a necessity, because Bruce had a six-and-a-half-hour drive from Glacier, would arrive late and would not have eaten. We could not leave until morning. We had to eat.

Our plan was to spend two days in the Spanish Peaks, the jagged, soaring mountains that form the northern section of the Madison Range. I lived almost at their feet. Whenever I took my eyes away from Lone Mountain, they occupied my view and my fantasies.

I had met Bruce two weekends earlier when I joined four members of the Montana Wilderness Association on a weekend backpack into the East Pioneer Range. The trip had gone nicely, although the morning after my return home I heard on the radio that a camper in Yellowstone, fifty miles down the road from where I lived, had been partially eaten by a grizzly.

Extremely strong, Bruce was a fast hiker, but willing to slow his pace for me. Knowing his own strength, he did not need wilderness to prove anything. He needed wilderness because he loved it. His spirit reminded me of the alpine guides I knew in Austria, men who had often been my companions in the Alps in those days before I married and settled in New York.

When my husband left, I spent months in a rage, alternating from murderous to suicidal. I wanted him to die, but I wouldn't have killed him for anything. I wouldn't go to jail for him. I'd done enough for him. He wasn't worth that. Anymore. He'd have to die on his own. But then, helpless in the face of his refusing to die, it seemed to me it was I who must. The world was too small to hold the two of us. When those moments happened I would rush to the bedroom, then clutch at the bed, terrified of letting go because letting go would give me access to the window or to the knives in the kitchen.

Over and over I saw my own fall from the window. I watched the fall as I had watched a friend fall from a climb. He had fallen a hundred and twenty feet. But his partner, my lover, held the rope, and although he was injured, his injuries healed. Climbing, after all, was not suicide. Just the opposite, an absolute affirmation of life, a glorying in it.

Over and over I felt a knife ripping into me, my hands guiding it, as if I were splitting open a chicken in the kitchen. I resented the image of the chicken, but I could not get rid of it. Once, in the worst of it, more terrified than ever, I suddenly thought I could *not* do it. I managed to telephone a friend, a psychotherapist who came at once.

"I thought maybe I wouldn't kill myself," I told him, "because I couldn't think of a way that didn't hurt. I thought that if I was concerned about pain, it was a sign I wouldn't do it."

"You might try cyanide," he suggested.

"I thought about it, but I didn't know where to get some."

"I think a hardware store," he said.

I hardly left the apartment. But then I flew to Montana in winter. As the plane approached the front range of the Rockies I knew that I would stay forever. It was only a matter of time before forever would begin.

The day before I left New York to begin the summer in Montana, a friend came for a drink. "You're not deliberately trying to set up an encounter with a grizzly, are you?" she asked. Although I felt braver in the face of bears than I had before getting the book assignment, I suspected that, to a bear, I would probably have appeared unchanged, which left me less than eager to go into Montana's mountains alone. I joined the Montana Wilderness Association at once and made arrangements to go on that East Pioneers trip with them. Early Saturday morning I drove two and a half hours to the meeting place where the leader waited.

We were to meet three others at a campground near the beginning of the route. When we reached the campground, they were waiting separately—a couple from Bozeman and a single man, Bruce, from East

Glacier, at the edge of Glacier National Park.

Bruce was dressed entirely in green. Thin, graying hair straggled out from under his green baseball cap. He smiled all the time and drove a white pickup. The hike leader threw our gear into the back of Bruce's truck, and we drove the remaining miles to the trail-head.

As we removed our gear, Bruce said, "Do you want to sleep in my tent so you don't have to carry yours?"

"Great," I answered.

It was not until we were actually on the trail that it occurred to me I had agreed to sleep in the tent of a strange man. How could I have been that lazy? I hate the weight that must be carried backpacking, but I am perfectly capable of carrying it. What would my laziness cost? I had often slept in a roomful of strange men in European mountain huts, lain perhaps between two men I had never even seen. But that's different. Sleeping with lots of strangers is different from sleeping with one. And this one looked so odd. All he did was smile and speak softly and walk, in his strength, ahead of the others. At our stops along the way I watched carefully for some sign of evil.

We reached our campsite in mid-afternoon, then took off on various private routes; the couple going one way, Bruce another, the leader and I yet another.

When the leader and I returned to camp late in the day, long after the other three, the male half of the couple said, "You look either worn out or totally stoned." I had not yet adjusted to Montana's altitude.

Bruce had the tent up and his stove going. "Would you like some hot chocolate?" he asked me as I unrolled my sleeping bag in the tent.

"Yes, please," I answered, feeling reassured. It seemed unlikely that a rapist would offer his victim hot chocolate.

In the morning I woke to the smell of coffee, real coffee, cowboy coffee, not the instant I, who despise instant, always carry backpacking. With instant coffee you don't have to wash the pot afterward. This seems an enormous advantage if it is I who must wash the pot.

"I've decided it's time to travel," he said. "See something besides Glacier."

"I thought I'd go into the Spanish Peaks the Fourth of July weekend," I said. "Do you want to come with me?"

Now I waited for him. Staring out the window at Lone Mountain, it occurred to me again that I knew nothing about him. He knew every wildflower. He was a photographer. He was the cook in the grammar school. He was a grease monkey on weekends. He had never been out of East Glacier. I knew nothing about him. I had slept in his tent, but there had been other people nearby.

"I'll come Friday night," he had said.

"You can sleep in my apartment," I had offered. Afterward I wondered, again, what I had done. Was it possible I was incapable of learning anything? The tent was one thing. How could I have invited a stranger to sleep in my apartment? He could be a murderer, any sort of pervert. The West is full of them. Men who seem likable, who smile all the time, who make hot chocolate for you, who bring you bear meat, who are full of violence. What do I do now? Nothing to be attractive, that's for sure. No makeup. Leave off my gold chain. In case he's a thief. Besides, it's sexy. No perfume. No candles on the table. There mustn't be anything romantic about the dinner. Dinner.

For some inexplicable reason, my husband phoned. It was the only time he did that summer. When I told him what had happened, he said, "Couldn't you just meet him for a drink?" My husband, of course, is a New Yorker.

I set the table, began planning the cooking, took a bread I'd baked days earlier from the freezer. I became as involved in the event of the dinner as I had just been in my fear. Then the fear returned. Then the event. At least it all canceled my husband. I checked the clock every few minutes. How long before he would arrive? What would it be like? How nice that a man was coming to dinner. Someone to make preparations for. Even if he would cook the bear, the rest was up to me. I had never cooked a bear. I'd never eaten one either. But it seemed appropriate. I thought that by ingesting bear I could ward off being ingested by bear. We become what we eat. I would become a bear. One bear rarely eats another bear. Eating bear would make me power-ful. Powerful enough to evade the violence I felt in Bruce? Why does he frighten me so much? His smile. His calmness. His eagerness to please. Would this be my last dinner? How could my husband have left me so defenseless, so open to anything? Who was here now to protect me? I had been so protected. Nothing could touch me so long as he existed. How was it he had phoned this particular day?

By ten o'clock Bruce had not yet arrived. I looked out the window into the parking lot, checked the table for the nineteenth time. The forks were still in place. And the wine glasses. At last, lights moved in the parking lot. A car stopped. A door closed. There was a knock on my door. I ran to it as if it were my husband. When I opened it, it was Bruce.

29

"Hi," he said.

"Hi," I said. "Come in."

"I made it in six hours," he said.

"Do you want a beer?"

At eleven he started cooking the bear meat. It was close to midnight when we ate and two o'clock by the time we went to bed, me in my bed in the sleeping alcove of the studio apartment, he on the floor, where I could see the foot of his sleeping bag but no more.

In the morning it was snowing. We abandoned the backpack, kept a fire going all day and sat talking, watching the sky. We talked about flowers. Bruce loved the mountain flowers. He photographed them. He dreamt of going to mountains where he'd heard a flower grew that he had never seen.

The apartment was small, but we did not crowd one another. When the sky cleared in the late afternoon we went for a walk, but turned back an hour later as clouds overran the sky, arriving home as a hailstorm broke. In the evening he took me into town for dinner. I liked riding in the truck. I thought people would think I was from Montana when they saw me sitting up there in the truck. Nobody would know I didn't belong here.

Later, we drank brandy in front of the fire, me on one side of the room, he on the other. I could feel him as if I were in his arms. I knew that if I just looked at him, he'd be there next to me. I kept my eyes from his. I did not want to start anything. It would have been so easy to start something, and so unfair, since, ultimately, I would not be there for him. I felt his vulnerability as if it were my own. He was not what I had thought he was, but some kind of saint, a pure soul for whom that smile is purity; that calmness and eagerness, innocence. He didn't know there was nothing. I knew I must not give him signals. I knew he felt the draw I felt. It was too powerful. I felt him feeling it. "I think I'll go to sleep," I said, finally. "Maybe tomorrow will be clear."

I went to bed, and he slept on the floor. I lay there thinking of him on the floor. It would be so easy, I thought, knowing he must be thinking the same.

Sunday morning dawned gray and wet, and neither of us wanted to go out into it. We sat in front of the fire until the afternoon cleared, then went for a drive in the truck. He stopped to pick wildflowers and gave them to me shyly. It was as if they were the first flowers I had ever been given, as if I were fifteen again and wearing a skirt. I had worn skirts in those days, mainly because the school required them. In those days I had felt that life was possible. When the sky clouded over we returned to the fire.

That night we once again slept separately. Lying

awake again, I thought I would only have to say his name. I used all my will to keep from saying it. It was as if we had entered into an agreement, drawn up a contract not to touch, not to acknowledge that our souls were locked in some inseparable embrace.

He had to leave by six in the morning to be at his job in Glacier by one. We breakfasted together as if we always did before he left for work. It was the kind of breakfast two people share when they will also share dinner at the end of the day.

"I'll leave the gun," he said, placing on the table the .44 pistol that he carried when backpacking in bear country. "So you can have some protection when you're alone in the wilderness. In case you meet a bear." He smiled.

"I'd probably only manage to make him mad," I said. "Then I'd really be in trouble. You better take it."

When it was time for him to go we embraced, as if there had been no contract not to touch; without shyness, as if we understood one another's arms.

When he left I missed him. The apartment was empty without him. Now that he was gone, we were lovers. Later in the day I remembered the gun. It had not even occurred to me that I could have used it on myself.

The Road to Wisdom

Georgette arrived in Montana the tenth of July to spend her summer holidays hiking with me. The trip I planned to make with her was through a little-used area I wanted to cover in my book—a nine-day trek down the Bitterroot Range, starting south of the Big Hole Battlefield. Much of it is trailless. Six separate U.S. Geological Survey maps cover the route.

Connecting in Dillon with Bob, the man who had led the East Pioneers hike, we would drive in two cars to Jackson, leave mine there so it would be available at the end, then continue to the start of the hike in his car. He would drop us off, joining us on the weekend, six days into our route. It was not until we were halfway between Dillon and Jackson, a distance of about forty-three miles, that I noticed my car needed gas. There are no gas stations between Dillon and Jackson. There is nothing between Dillon and Jackson but the rolling hills and broad flats of the wind-scoured Big Hole Valley. Cattle graze across the valley's wide expanse. Beaverslides, the haystackers designed by two Big Hole ranchers in 1907, lean like giant ladders against the sky. The Bitterroot Range sweeps along to the west in a series of wavelike peaks. A snowstorm the day before had blanketed the land with white. The sky pressed gray and heavy on it. There were no cars on the road. There was nothing off the road but a thousand head of cattle and the cold, rolling space.

The gas gauge had registered empty for thirty miles by the time we reached Jackson, where the town street was closed. There is one paved road in Jackson, a section of the highway from Dillon to Wisdom, about twelve miles north of Jackson. It continues from Wisdom north through the Big Hole, where it arches around the northern end of the Pioneers and heads east to Interstate 15, and west to the Big Hole Battlefield. The sole paved road in the Big Hole Valley, it has been paved for only a few years. It was closed now in Jackson for an annual festival. The festival spread through most of the town, which consists of Rose's Cantina, a general store, a garage with a gas pump and, across the road, a post office in the entranceway to a white frame house and the sprawling Jackson Hot Springs Hotel. The gas pump was closed for the festival. Traffic, of which we were the only example, was being rerouted east of the paved road, through the rutted, deep, slippery mud of the old bypass behind town.

The local inhabitants, bundled up against the damp cold, promenaded the few yards of town, eating sandwiches and drinking beer. A few sat on the porch of the hotel, a few others on the porch of Rose's Cantina, where they seemed to be waiting for John Huston to come and direct them.

We backtracked a mile to leave the car, which apparently runs without gas, in the yard of someone Bob knew, then transferred our gear into his station wagon. At that time he offered to put gas in the car before meeting us on the weekend, and suggested I give him the key.

On our way again, we turned west before Wisdom to begin a forty-mile drive on a forest service dirt road. In fields bordering the road, the cattle stood still against the wind. We passed a few cabins, shacks, an occasional trailer. The day remained gray. We were dropped off at a place that might have been anywhere, it seemed so arbitrary, that spot, as if Bob had merely tired of the drive. "I think that's the way," he said, pointing out a direction.

Lifting our heavy packs onto our backs—we carried enough food and gear for ten days—we started up a dirt road. A few hundred feet later it descended into Idaho. Here we turned away from it, entering the forest, plunging into knee-high snow, often tripping over buried, blown-down trees that had been collecting for a hundred years. The slow, long climb up the forest brought us to open slopes where the going became easier. But it was late now. We had expected to do ten miles. We made about three.

An evening sun appeared as we set up camp in a broad park. There was space for the tent beneath a tree where the earth had been sheltered from snow. Once it was up I noticed a pile of clean bones nearby. Georgette noticed it too, but neither of us mentioned it to the other until the next day.

It had probably just been a coyote that had cleaned those bones, a coyote and months of weather. Certainly it was not a bear. We had seen no bear sign. Nevertheless, the sight of it made me think we should make our presence known. Since reading Farley Mowat's *Never Cry Wolf* several years earlier, I had been impressed by how logically and easily a man, as well as a wolf, can mark his territory. I now felt that even without being men we should mark ours. After all, maybe I'd just missed some bear sign. Bear country was new to me. If they were here, would they respect our claim? Would a technique borrowed from wolves work with bears? Was there at least that much commonality among animals? Could we be included?

I suggested to Georgette that she pee in whatever sort of line she could manage, somewhere on the far side of the tent.

"I'll do this side," I added.

"Are you sure?" she asked, with an odd look on her face. I shrugged off the look. "It worked for Farley Mowat," I said.

This did not seem particularly reassuring to her, but she did as she was told. I'm not sure it was the effectiveness of Farley Mowat she was questioning.

No doubt any animal watching (I believe there are *always* animals watching in the wild) found us behaving even more oddly than people ordinarily do. This is not a moment for self-consciousness, I thought at the time. Let them think what they will. On the other hand, I felt silly. I discovered that it is not easy to pee properly when you're giggling. Also, I felt penis envy for the first time in my life. But it must have worked, because no bears came.

* *

Morning dawned crisp and clear, one of those clean Montana mornings that inspire movement, life, hope and adventure. We packed up and continued across the park, descending into a narrow ravine, then up out of it onto the rough and rubbly loose stones of a scree slope. A traverse was necessary, but Georgette headed directly up instead.

It's easier to go up steep slopes than across them. Facing in, the slope itself providing security by its very nearness to one's body, one is unmindful of the steepness below. Traversing, it seems as if the slope, instead of offering protection, will simply send one hurtling off into space. A false step on a traverse, even on a comfortable slope, seems to promise a fall; a long, steep way down; the impossibility of stopping; the abyss. Going straight up may be harder on one's heart and lungs, but appearing to offer safety, it is easier on one's mind. Climbing is as much an exercise of the mind as of the body.

There also seems to be some sort of human instinct toward up. New skiers have no trouble turning upward, into the hill, but often have a difficult time making themselves turn downward. In skiing, "up" stops you. In climbing, up sometimes seems the only possible direction.

"You're climbing up too far," I said.

"I'm frightened of scree," she answered.

"I thought you'd done some mountaineering," I said.

"I always had trouble with scree, though."

There is a country song that, slightly altered, now embedded itself in my mind: "You picked a fine time to tell me, Georgette . . . "

I stood directly below her on the slope so I could stop her if she slipped, the song playing over and over in my head. The sun was hot on the dusty scree. Too much time later, we left the slope to climb onto a shoulder of Sheep Mountain, a long, snow-covered trapezoid, the first real mountain along the route. According to our map, we should cross over the shoulder to the far side and a small lake, the only water for miles. Our goal as a campsite the previous day, it was where we would camp tonight. Tomorrow we would retrace our steps to the side we were now on, then continue the route by traversing below the summit. We stopped for lunch on the shoulder.

By now I understood Georgette was truly terrified of scree, and nervous as well at not being on a trail. We had often hiked together in New York's mountains, and I knew how strong and capable she was, but now realized her fear could cause an accident her ability did not warrant. If it was necessary for me to go for help, being left alone would be ghastly for her. Help was a good distance away. If something happened to me, it would be hard for her to go. There was much more scree ahead. I knew we should turn back.

I didn't want to. The Montana summer is short. I needed this route for my book. In all likelihood there would be no other time to do it if we abandoned it now. I resented being thrown into the quandary of choosing what was right—turning back—over what was necessary for my book—going on.

"Georgette, we don't have to go on, but you'll have to make the decision. You tell me how you feel about it. If you're too frightened, we'll just turn back."

This was an awful thing to do to her. You cannot ask someone who is frightened to make a decision involving someone else. Alone, if you are frightened, you can always turn back. No one sees you. No one depends on you. You have not interfered with anyone else's life. Alone I have often turned back from routes that frightened me. With others, never.

"I know when I've done it, I'll be pleased," she said, "but . . . do you have my mother's address? Just in case . . . "

This question, which one usually assumes is a joke, was a serious question. We started out. A few yards from the lunch site we reached a short scree slope, a traverse. I told Georgette to go first so I could see her if she got into difficulty. She started out. Her knees were shaking. I know what it's like when your knees shake. It has happened to me rock climbing. There is nothing you can do about it except make the next move, commit yourself to moving, move quickly enough so that you move out of the shaking. Sometimes you cannot move out of the shaking. Sometimes you just want to cry.

"We're going back," I said.

"Why?" she asked, her whole body registering relief when we stepped off the scree.

"Because there's too much snow ahead and we don't have the proper equipment. I don't want to take a chance."

Rather than retrace our steps over the first scree slope, we made our way farther up the ravine, climbing out of it on a steeper but less rubbly incline, to camp on a green bench lavish with wildflowers.

The following day we continued to the park of our first night and beyond it to the hill we had reached from the woods the first day. There was no trace of snow. Lupine, larkspur, sedum and a hundred other wildflowers sprouted in clumps and mats out of the short grass and among the rocks. Sunday's route, over

41

the blowdowns, was also snow-free. The snow had hidden much of the grid of blowdowns from us and had made the walking easier. Now, moving forward, lifting one leg over a log, then the other, taking a small step, then another lift up and over, was exhausting.

We reached the road about one o'clock. The sun was high and summer-hot. The sandy road reflected it back so that heat beat down at us from above and swelled up at us from below. My anger at abandoning the route wrapped me as the heat did.

I said nothing. What could I have said?

We had walked about five miles when two cars approached, one after the other, both going the wrong way. A Volkswagen with Connecticut plates contained two ladies delighted, although not astounded, to find two other eastern ladies in the middle of nowhere. That's what they called it, the middle of nowhere. They wanted very much to chat about the adventure of taking a back and almost unused road to Idaho.

Shortly afterward a pickup carrying two men and a woman, trappers who lived in a shack down the road, rumbled up. "You've got about thirty-five miles to Wisdom," the driver offered. Other than that, they didn't have much to say.

A forest service truck passed, going our direction,

but did not stop. They are not allowed to pick up hitch-hikers. They *are* allowed to talk to them. Ahead of us, a black bear crossed the road, followed by two cubs. One of the cubs sat down in the road to watch us. Most likely he had never seen two women with backpacks before. His mother returned to the road and somehow must have called him, because he jumped up and ran after her. We decided to sing so we wouldn't surprise the sow if she doubled back to the road. "Frère Jacques" was the only song we had in common. We sang loudly in the heat and dust of the Montana road.

Once we were beyond the spot where the bears had crossed, Georgette's long, strong stride carried her rapidly ahead of me. I watched the distance between us grow. The sun beat down in the space between us with a white heat. Each step was a step farther into it. Cattle grazed along the side of the road and stood in the creeks, a few lifting their heads as I passed. Calves, frightened, bolted back from the roadsides as I approached. We were out of water. The cows in the creeks made me doubly aware of how thoroughly we were out of water. There were so many miles to go and so slight a chance of a ride. We would have to camp in these pastures full of cow dung and ruined creeks. Dismay and fury slowed my pace. I forced myself faster; forced myself to keep going at all. It was too hot.

I was too thirsty. I was tired of this unshaded road that would go on forever. It was too far to Wisdom.

Then it occurred to me that it is always a long way to Wisdom. But here I was, actually walking down the road toward it. How many people even know there is an honest-to-God road they can take to get there? Built by the U.S. Department of Agriculture Forest Service and accessible to any of the American public who cares to travel an inordinate distance to get to it. It was built with my tax money.

I straightened up. My weariness left. I walked, exulting.

Now that my mind was freed to go its own routes, the hot sun and the sandy road reminded me of another walk. When I was three years old, my cousins and I had gone to the beach with our mothers. Kayla, three years my senior, and I wandered away from the others into the park along the beach. We were on a dirt road. We wandered far enough to get lost, although "lost" was not yet a part of my vocabulary. I thought we were on an adventure, but Kayla was old enough to understand that we were lost. When we talked about it as adults, Kayla told me that I was happy being lost, that I was content just to walk along our way forever, but that she knew enough to be scared. No one seems to know how we were found. Recently I asked my mother and she had no idea. "You were always getting lost," she said.

Was that the last time I was not afraid? Until now. On this road I was not afraid. Walk all night? Fine. Sleep in a cow pasture? Fine. Be thirsty, hot, hungry? Fine. These were all external things. They could not harm me. We were safely off Sheep Mountain. Was it some instinct of Georgette's that, expressing itself as fear, allowed us to turn back? Was she "old" enough to be afraid while I, childishly selfish, off on my adventure, did not know enough to sense some danger ahead— some danger in bad weather or unfamiliar terrain; the danger that I had undertaken too big a venture with too little thought; the danger of leading wrong some-one too dependent on me; the danger that one way or another I would mess up?

But there is always that danger. What is necessary is to risk. Is it the conflict between my own need for safety and my own need to risk that results in my own particular fear? Needing safety, I am afraid to risk. Yet needing safety, I know with every fibre of my soul the necessity of risking. Rushing to any available edge, over and over and over. Pushing myself, forever, away from that place that seems safe. Safety is an illusion. Risk is real. It's better to deal with something real.

That is, ultimately, the only "safety."

Looking up, I saw Georgette standing in front of a trailer a few yards ahead, waving at me.

"We've been invited for coffee," she called, smiling delightedly. Her smile is joyous. I understood how I loved her.

Inside the trailer a grizzled, rumpled old man poured coffee. A prospector from Utah who had spent nineteen summers here, he was eager to talk, to show us his gold, to present us his life. "This land is worth six million dollars," he said. "I would take you to town, but I have to wait for some people."

I was glad of the coffee. Georgette was charmed by the adventure. Still, we both turned to look out the window at every sound, on the off-chance someone might be driving by. I knew there was no way to be out of the trailer and onto the road in time to stop an approaching vehicle, but it was instinctive to look anyway. I apologized to the old man for continually looking, which seemed rude, as if he could not hold my full attention.

"But it would be nice if we caught someone going by," I explained.

"You have too little faith," he said.

Yes, I thought, he's right. When it's time for a ride, the driver will appear. In the meantime, we'll continue walking down this road. That calmed me. Something in me truly hoped we would walk through the night. I think what I really wanted was that the road last the rest of my life.

Kayla died at forty-two, twelve years after cancer was diagnosed. Although she was so ill most of the time that the doctors could not understand how she was even alive, she would not allow the disease to master her. At a time when the doctors wanted her in a wheelchair and close to the hospital, she rented a house in the country and went out for a walk. In the course of it she became exhausted and had to lie down on the ground. She rested, but could not then stand by herself.

"I was frightened at first," she told me later, "but then I thought, what would Ruthie do . . . ? [Only Kayla and her father ever called me that.] I decided you would move calmly and slowly and patiently and you would make your way, as if there was no limit on time. If I couldn't stand up, I could crawl. I crawled slowly to the house. I used the door to pull myself up. I felt triumphant."

When it seemed time to leave, the old man followed us outside. We lifted our packs, which we had left leaning against his truck, to swing them onto our backs.

"Put them in the truck," he said.

"But you're waiting for someone," I reminded him.

"They'll wait for me," he said.

We threw the packs into the back of the truck, climbed in next to him and reached Wisdom before five in the afternoon. He let us off at a rickety motel where the water smelled. Later, discovering the only functioning light bulb was in the bathroom, we used our flashlights for the first time on the trip.

Wisdom is larger than Jackson. There are actually a couple of motels, the Antler Bar which is decorated with many paintings of the Antler Bar, a restaurant with another bar attached, a general store, post office, gas station and forest service district office. There are many more houses in town and a larger school. I headed directly for the forest service office to ask if there were some mountains around without scree on them. The ranger suggested going to the lake where we had arranged to meet Bob on Friday. It was now Tuesday.

The ranger's route required a twenty-mile drive to reach the trailhead. The drive passed through Jackson, twelve miles away. We could have hitched a ride to Jackson with no problem and picked up my car, except I couldn't use it since Bob had taken the key.

I have a friend in Paris, an authority on transportation, who had once worked with Governor Judge (when he was governor the first time around) to develop a public transit system for Montana. This seemed to me a good time to implement one. At this moment, Jackson was about as accessible as Paris.

We went to the restaurant for dinner. The waitress told us the special was fried chicken. I asked her if there was someone we could hire to drive us to the trailhead.

"My boyfriend," she suggested. "He works for the forest service, but he's off tomorrow."

I phoned him from the bar. That was not how he wanted to spend his day off and suggested we ask the waitress.

When I returned, Georgette had a strange look on her face. I realized at once she had read the notebook I had left lying on the table after making notes about the trip during dinner. I should have considered that her view of friendship was one that assumes access to all that belongs to a friend. She, in turn, holds nothing back. For her there are no secrets, no silences between friends.

"I thought you said we were turning back because of the snow," she said.

"We turned back because it didn't make sense to

risk an accident," I said.

In the notebook I had written it as it had happened. At that moment on the scree slope, the snow had seemed a good excuse, a way to save face for a friend. It had nothing to do with turning back. There really wasn't enough snow to be worrisome. Now, seeing Georgette's distress that I had not been straight with her, and believing that it had not been her fear that had turned us back, I wondered whose face it was I was saving.

What difference did that particular route make to me anyway? The route could be changed for the book. The pages were blank. If I did not use one map, I could use another. The book would be what I made it. Every book is made. Nothing can be lacking that is not put in.

I had had a few trepidations about the trip, so much of it trailless, all of it new to me and completely unfamiliar to her. Who knows what turning back saved us? There are reasons our routes work out the way they do. There is a degree to which I must be willing to choose my own path; a greater degree to which I must be ready to follow the path that reveals itself to me.

As for the specific trip with Georgette . . . now, I felt, we would be able to start.

Mountain Man

A notice in the weekly paper announced a two-day course in tracking to be given by a local mountain man in late July. The first half would take place on the campus of Montana State University in Bozeman, the second in Yellowstone Park. The mountain man's name was Fred. He had a Ph.D. in geography, a passion for Native American tradition, and a small condominium with his wife in the same complex at the base of Lone Mountain where I rented mine. I suppose that in the early days of Montana he would have lived in a tipi or a log hut and might not have known how to read. I had not met him before the course.

The mystique of the mountain men draws me. The real mountain men. Those nineteenth-century trappers who, wild and fierce as the country they traveled, left their spirit forever on the Rocky Mountains. For them, survival depended on their own skill, wits and luck, on nature and the friendliness of Indians. Some Indians traded with them. Some mated with them. Some preferred to kill them. Hard times were the norm. The harder they were, the better the stories. Mountain men legends are full of trappers making their way through hundreds of miles of difficult, un-familiar country, possibly barefoot, nude, disarmed or in some similar disarray, usually in a blizzard after an encounter with a grizzly bear or a band of Indians. The best of them, the Jim Bridgers and Joe Meeks and Jedediah Smiths, survived well, explored and mapped the uncharted mountains, and made the fur compa-nies employing them rich. They never made them-selves rich. But money wasn't what mattered. Free-dom mattered. Wildness mattered.

Besides Fred, there are still other mountain men around, men versed in the old skills who use their lives in longing for that time they missed. They make them-selves buckskin outfits and trappers' cloaks and moccasins. At the rendezvous held each summer—reenactments of the yearly camps where the trappers met to resupply and get in a year's worth of carous-ing—you can hardly tell them from their nineteenth-century counterparts. It's their pickup trucks and Hondas that give them away.

Once, on a rainy morning in Wyoming's Wind River Mountains, I came upon a man in buckskin tending his horses in a meadow. He and his lady had set up camp at its edge and had a warm fire going in spite of the rain. I was cold, and they offered me tea. They were spending the summer in the mountains. The two of them and three horses. He showed me how to use tinder to start a fire in the rain.

The problem with being a mountain man today is that it's not a full-time job. Paved roads, jet airplanes, fur farms and an increasingly diminishing wilderness are not conducive to it. A mountain man with time on his hands might as well learn to read and get advanced degrees. At least a degree in geography keeps one in touch with the land.

Nine of us—seven men, my friend Susanna, visiting from New York, and I—gathered in a classroom in a modern red-brick building on campus. The chairs on which we sat were yellow, red and blue plastic, as in a kindergarten or a hospital waiting room. Ill-contained in that space, Fred leaned uneasily against the edge of the teacher's desk. Tall and slender, his mane of blond curls and full blond beard made him seem too broad, too large for a room with plastic chairs. He wore a plaid shirt, jeans and cowboy boots and spoke in a soft voice. Almost immediately we moved outdoors into the easy summer morning, arranging ourselves comfortably against the brick of Wilson Hall. A Saturday morning in midsummer; there was no one else on campus. On the manicured lawn, Fred talked about playing with wild animals. He had been a student of the tracker Tom Brown, whose own initiation into the ways of wild things had been at the hand of an American Indian in New Jersey's Pine Barrens.

I know the Pine Barrens a little; well enough to understand how only the people born there can know them well. Miles and miles of flat sandy forest and bog are rent everywhere by streams. Dirt roads crisscross the region in a maze only the Pineys can unravel. The roads never lead out, but farther and deeper into this wild place. I have heard there are people in the Pine Barrens who have not been out of them. I have walked miles on its sandy earth and camped on it, swum some of its streams, feasted on its blueberries, which are the best in the world, paid my respects on the spot to the Mexican pilot who crashed and died there on some early, daring flight.

I have also read Tom Brown's books and now thought of his description of playing with a wild badger. Wanting

something so much he had become it, Fred had incorporated his teacher.

The day grew warmer. The sun slid down the side of
the building. We moved forward, into the shade of
trees, all of us earnestly taking notes as if the notes
would show us something. The sky was blue. A slight
breeze fluttered through the trees. Morning spread
over the empty lawns. Fred's voice faded in and out of
the light. I remembered how much I hated school. It
was not studying I hated but the walls that enclosed
me. Outside the walls there was the sky. The trick was
to get to it. Now, listening to Fred, we were outside, so
I realized that even the voice of the teacher keeps one
from the sky. I forced myself to his voice.

"Splatter vision," he was saying, "means to pick a
point, then extend it a hundred eighty degrees. Look
for movement in the space, return to the point, expand
another hundred eighty degrees." We stretched our
arms out to the sides at shoulder level to illustrate to
ourselves our hundred-eighty-degree field of vision. I
liked this. It helped wonderfully to reduce the strain of
sitting cross-legged on the ground and listening. It
seemed a position for flight.

"Soft eyes means not focusing on anything, but
seeing everything at once," he continued. "Look for
patterns, connections, movements." *Ochachonya*, ran

through my mind. Dark eyes. *Ochagrostnya*. The Russian song my Russian mother sang to me as a child.

"Once an animal is seen," Fred went on, "focus on the environment. What are other animals, shrubbery, trees, wind, everything surrounding the animal, doing?"

He called this bio-grammar. I was startled by the use of a word to explain what we were doing. "Splatter vision" and "soft eyes" seemed too physical to be words, but now Fred had become the scientist applying language to instinctive reaction; the teacher speaking; the mountain man lost in the classroom. But the grass lies a certain way when an elk has made a bed of it, I thought, whether one describes it or not.

Language for describing ways of seeing, even when exact, seems arbitrary. It is always language; a description. A description is not seeing, just as a name is not the flower. But language helps you feel better. It provides the illusion you know something. Do you know more if you know the name but have never seen the flower; if you have seen the flower but have not heard its name? Language also exists when no one hears it, which is why it is an ideal tool for teachers whose students' souls are elsewhere.

Not that I would argue with learning techniques for seeing. They are not instinctive for everyone, but are a necessity in successful tracking. You could track from here to the Kalahari, but unless you know how to look for whatever is hiding at the end of the tracks, you'd never be much besides a sort of abstract tracker, someone who tracked for the tracks rather than the animal. I suppose this is not unreasonable if one loves tracks but hates animals.

"There is seeing by knowing habits," Fred said. "Knowing an animal is out there—an owl in a tree, for example—because of the owl pellets at the foot of the tree. You simply look in the tree for the owl." See the owl. Run, Spot, run. Run to the owl, Spot. Easy, boy. Do not eat the owl. You'll get some Alpo later. Do not be eaten by the owl. Be a big enough dog, Spot.

Picking a point on the far horizon, then drawing a line of vision in a straight line from oneself to the horizon, Fred called "horizon-seeing." He did not go into seeing beyond the horizon, but most likely that falls under the heading of religion rather than tracking.

It seemed appropriate that these thoughts on seeing were followed by an exercise in which we were blindfolded. We were told to walk to a tree which we had studied before our blindfolds were put on. Would we walk in a straight line or veer left or right of the tree? Each one of us veered one direction or another, although some of us more than others. "People naturally walk in circles," Fred announced.

I had ended considerably to the left of the tree. But I have a tendency to choose left over right. If I come to a fork in a trail, for instance, and am not certain which is the correct one, I invariably go left. (This is not invariably correct.) I tend to look left before looking right, to step first with my left foot. When I told Fred about this he suggested heading for the tree again, this time overcompensating to the right. When the blindfold was removed, I stood directly in front of the tree. Will this be of use someday in the forest? Will it keep me from walking in circles if I am lost? Will it affect me politically?

"How much can you learn from one track? " Fred asked. "Age? Sex? What the animal was doing? Every track is a unique combination of the animal, the terrain, the weather." He suggested we make a track of our own in a box, then watch what happens to it over twenty-four to forty-eight hours, in different weather. I liked the idea of keeping my own track in a box. Would I then be able to see where it ultimately led?

Leaving the cool of the shade, we removed our shoes to make tracks in the powdery gray dust that edges the cement walks crossing the campus grass. Each of us chose a spot, then took a few steps in it. My feet were directly in a line, but only four toes showed on each. The track of my right foot was fainter than that of my left, the toes of my left foot more defined than those of my right. Is my left foot more definite because it gets more use, or does it get more use because it is more definite? Is this something I need to know? Can I be right-handed and left-footed?

The following day Susanna and I drove with Fred and Phil, a friend from Big Sky, to Yellowstone to meet the rest of the group for some actual tracking. On the drive through the canyon, we saw two moose and one coyote. Reaching the park ahead of schedule, we stopped at one of Phil's favorite fishing spots. The fields backing away from the stream were covered by buffalo dung, some old, some recent. There were no animals. We arrived at the meeting place, a small museum, to find that several of the group, while waiting, had seen a black bear down the slope from the museum.

We waded knee-deep across a river, our shoes in our hands, feeling with our toes for the slippery rocks. On the far side we dried our feet with our socks, put our shoes back on. Fred wore high deerskin moccasins he had made. In his fascination with the ways of Native Americans, he spends much of his time curing and tanning skins (which, no hunter, he buys), then sewing shirts and pants, jackets and moccasins and shields. They are often elaborately beaded or quilled. Most people in the area who pass a dead porcupine on the road immediately call Fred so he can collect the quills. To cure the skins he must let them lie soaking for a period of time. Aside from the smell of it, the practicality of it in a small apartment with only one bathroom certainly requires a commitment to the art. The process could be speeded up, but, as Fred says, "It takes longer because my wife refuses to chew the skins."

It fascinates me that he will not hunt.

Without hunting, the mountain man would have starved. His diet, like that of the Indians among whom he lived, was meat; the game that was abundant then; the game in whose absence he went hungry; the game whose meat gave him strength and energy enough to pursue a life with no ease; the game he, like the Indian, honored because it kept him alive.

Of course, no one needs to hunt these days. The supermarkets are full of dead meat. Who, I wonder, cutting into a piece of cow, asks its forgiveness? Yet the cow is dead and we may as well eat it. Eating it does it more honor than allowing it to rot, whether we ask its forgiveness or not. Most modern-day mountain men *do* hunt in their need to maintain a tradition, although the tradition, now, may be beside the point. Killing the meat you mean to eat at least allows the animal its natural place in the life chain; allows it not to have been raised for the slaughterhouse; allows you to confront your own responsibility for its death. In the face of this, some people become vegetarians. But I see no dishonor in hunting wherever the animal is truly used. Daughter of a hunter, I grew up on game birds. My father loved the birds as much as he loved his hunting dog and the autumn fields. Even as a child I knew we did not take the bird before us on the table for granted.

Yet Fred, mountain man, buys his meat at the grocery.

We entered woods, checking each tree for claw marks, shreds of hair where some animal had rubbed, worn places on the bark. We looked closely at the path to see if a pebble had been turned over, a tuft of grass laid flat, a fresh footprint left, an old footprint spread and softened by weather and time. We noticed which grasses had been nibbled, where an elk had made a bed. Although we did not voice it, all of us were looking for bear sign, pretending more interest than we felt in whatever else we came across, while longing for a sign of the great one, the white bear, old silver-tip, the mighty griz; longing for a sign of him and sight of him too, but at a good distance; sight of him ambling up some distant hillside, ambling away from us. We would have been satisfied with a black bear, but a grizzly would be a coup, the great reward. I was aware, as we made our slow way through the woods and out into the open space of a meadow, of what was around me in every direction. This was Yellowstone, the bear's country. That bear I have so feared, I seek. I am still frightened, but I am different. Instead of crippling me, the fear now fills me with awe.

In the forest again, we came out onto a stream. There were swans on it and a hawk perched on a log. The group dispersed. Susanna, Phil and I made our own way. I was less easy in the woods than in the meadow, where my range of vision encompassed more. On the other hand, the forest is full of trees to climb. "This is dangerous," Phil said. "We should stay together. There could be a grizzly."

Some part of me wanted to be alone in the wildness of the place; some part of me still descending from wildness. There must be that in each of us; some part of us that urges us deeper into the forest when we know it is time to turn around. We are separated from our origins in it by about a million seventy-five thousand years, not a long time in the memory of the earth. But what of our own memories? How much can we remember of our inherited wariness? How much sharper are all my senses in the forest?

No grizzly came. We rejoined the others shortly before the river and waded across, the spot deeper than our earlier crossing. The water came up to my thighs. On the far side a huge group of tourists had gathered at the edge of the road. We saw them first, then, beyond them, their reason for gathering—a herd of elk standing in the meadow they faced. There seemed to be hundreds of elk. We had spent all day looking for animals. Here, before us, was a prime rule for tracking in national parks: the surest sign of animals is a traffic jam.

The River

In October I moved away from Lone Mountain and into a log cabin in the Gallatin Canyon. The land backed up behind it directly into the Gallatin Range, about ninety miles of mountains that filed north from Yellowstone Park to Bozeman. Mule deer came down from the forested mountains to the salt lick I placed for them. On sunny days a pair of marmots came out from the rocks partway up the slope to lie on a large stump in the sun. The front windows looked out on the Madison Range. At night I would lie in bed listening to coyotes sing from the rolling meadows at the foot of the Madisons.

Although there were periodic snows from early autumn on, winter moved in unequivocally in early November. A cold spell hit before Christmas. The temperature dropped to forty-six degrees below zero and stayed there ten days. In my log cabin the toilet froze. After that, the car had to be towed to the wrecker's garage to be warmed enough to start. Next, the water pipes in the sink froze. When the landlord came to check the pipes, he bumped into icicles hanging from the roof of the cabin, sending them crashing into the plastic carefully put up as storm windows. On two windows, the plastic, brittle from the cold, shattered. Frost immediately mounted up the panes, rendering the wood stove I used to heat the cabin almost ineffective. Ice crystals hung on the air, an ethereal veil over the clear, ice-blue sky. If you went outside and breathed, your nostrils stuck together. Life became basic. You attended to chores that allowed you to survive. If you had other plans, you put them aside. I began to understand that, in Montana, you do not do things on your own time but on nature's.

Even when the extreme cold broke and the temperature shot up to zero, you still could not just up and do something, like go to a movie or get papers Xeroxed. Town was an hour's drive, via thirty twisting miles, from the cabin. Roads might be too icy to drive, or closed by seventy-mile-an-hour winds whipping blinding snow across them. A blizzard could be raging, or nighttime cold could make car trouble on the lonely road lethal. I stocked up on groceries and typing paper, so rarely needed to make the trip.

Early April brought warm days when the air felt soft with spring, even if actual spring doesn't appear up here in the mountains until June. The road was occasionally clear of ice and snow. The local bears began to come out of their winter dens. The bighorn sheep prepared to return to the heights after wintering in the canyon. I, too, felt stirrings in my blood, that restlessness, precursor of change, that rises in everything living in spring. Although out of the habit of change, preferring to sit in my cabin and work on the book I came to Montana to write, I had already adapted to getting into the car and having it (1) actually start, and (2) get me where I wanted to go.

One morning I wanted to go to Lone Mountain Ranch in Big Sky, where the second day of a two-day Nor-Am ski race was being held. This was an official FIS cross-country race, suddenly transferred to the ranch from Calgary because there was no snow in Canada. The ranch, a rustic but luxurious cross-country ski center and resort, with miles of superb trails, had had only two weeks to prepare for the race.

I intended to take photos to go with an article I'd written for the *High Country Independent Press*, a local weekly. The senior men's race, the one in which I was

chiefly interested, was a fifteen-kilometer event beginning at ten o'clock, and the racer I wanted to photo-
graph, Pierre Harvey, was Canada's fastest cross-
country skier. He was the only male cross-country
skier Canada sent to the Olympics in Sarajevo. Pierre
is also a bicycle racer who had competed in the 1976
Summer Olympics. He was supposed to go to Moscow
in 1980, but along with the other Canadian and American athletes, was knocked out by the boycott. Ten-
twenty was his start time. It would take me about
twenty minutes to drive to the start from my cabin, up
the narrow road that winds along the Gallatin River.

I planned to leave the cabin at nine forty-five. As I
walked toward the car, a pickup truck pulled into the
driveway, blocking it. Two men jumped out and started
running back up the road. It was snowing. It had been
snowing all night.

"I have to get out in a minute," I called to them. One
turned around, hesitated, then started toward me.

"There's a car in the river," he shouted.

"Keep going then," I called back. "I'll phone the
sheriff."

The woman who answered the phone in the sheriff's office asked if anyone was hurt and where was it
exactly and what was my name. There are no street
addresses here. You describe where things are by the

number of miles from some known point. She said she'd send someone right away. I went back to the front of the house. The two men who left the pickup were coming back now. Everybody in the car in the river was all right, they said; other people were helping them. In the meantime, however, a van had turned over in the ditch on the other side of the road, near where the car had gone into the river.

At that moment a young man appeared, shakily walking down the road. "I have to call a wrecker," he said.

"Come inside."

When he came in, I could see how ashen he looked and told him to sit down. I called the garage. The wrecker had been at the cabin the day before when some visiting friends from Billings were leaving and their car slid off the driveway into the ditch.

The man at the garage asked if anyone was hurt. I asked the young man now sitting on the couch with his head buried in his hands.

"We're all right," he said. "My friend and the dog are all right."

As he left, a Bronco or Ram or Jeep, or whatever those expensive vehicles are that all Westerners who don't drive either pickups or Subarus drive, pulled into the driveway.

Two men with beards sat in front, and three women, all shaking, in the back. The women had been in the river. "Do you want to come inside by the fire? " I asked, thinking it was probably warmer in the car. The fire is just the small wood-burning stove that heats the cabin. One of the men said he thought they could stay in the car for a while. I went back inside.

A few minutes later the men brought the three women in, two in their twenties and one in her fifties. One of the young women, whose name was Kailene, kept saying, "Oh, Mom, I'm so sorry . . . " The other, Linée, did not speak. They were both wet up to their waists. Kailene's mother, Donna, who spoke calmly but could not stop shaking, kept trying to reassure her. Then she turned to me and said she had to call her friend in Belgrade.

Belgrade is about forty miles up the canyon road from me; that is, in winter, about an hour's drive. The *High Country Independent Press* is published there. The women had been on their way from Belgrade to West Yellowstone, another fifty miles south on the canyon road. Kailene and Linée live in West, as they call it out here.

Kailene and Donna had planned to leave on a two-week trip to California the next day. Linée had been persuaded to come along on this overnight visit to

Donna's friends, Erlene and Hank, in Belgrade. Erlene told Donna on the phone that they would be right out. I couldn't help overhearing Donna's end of the conversation and, after she hung up, realized she hadn't told Erlene where they were, other than in the Gallatin River. I called Erlene back to tell her that the cabin was a mile south of Karst.

Erlene knew just where that was, because over thirty years earlier she had been a wrangler for Karst, which was a dude ranch then, as well as a favorite watering spot of the fishermen who came, and still come, to cast flies into the blue-ribbon Gallatin. Before that, Karst had been a stage stop on the long trip from Bozeman to Yellowstone Park.

Linée began to cry, and one of the two men who had picked up the women on the road after they'd clambered out of the river held her until she finished.

Kailene continued to apologize to her mother. "I couldn't do anything else . . . ," she said over and over.

"It wasn't your fault," her mother would say each time.

When Linée stopped crying, the two men left. At that point a pair of medics arrived in a bright red car from Big Sky, fifteen miles away. One of them was the telephone man who had installed my phone (also red) when I moved into the cabin. He had given me advice on how many cords of wood I would need to get through the winter. I have auxiliary electric heat, but because that is expensive, I had planned to heat just by the wood stove. The other was a carpenter currently building new luxury condominiums at the foot of Lone Mountain. They brought in blankets and medical supplies, took everybody's blood pressure, asked many questions and were very kind. Once they made sure the women were all right, the medics went back up the road to see if the second set of medics, those who had gone to see about the men in the van, needed help.

Soon after they left, a highway patrolman arrived. He was not particularly pleasant, offering not a single sympathetic word. This struck me as odd, because the few police I'd personally met since I'd been in Montana had been extremely nice. Even one who gave me a ticket for speeding (it cost five dollars) did not call me by my first name. He pointed out that I could pay on the spot and added that he had clocked me going seventy-one miles per hour up a hill on Interstate 90. I was actually rather proud of my little Subaru for being able to do that. When he left he wished me a good day. I felt as if he were a tour guide. But this man, while perfectly polite, was a cold fish, oblivious to the fact that the women were literally shaking with fear and confusion.

After he left, the medics checked back to see that the women were still all right and, when they left, Erlene and Hank turned up from Belgrade, with their friend Lonny. That made all of them feel better. Erlene said that when the phone rang, the last thing she had expected was Donna calling to tell her they were in the river.

It was now about noon. Of course, I had missed the race. And lost the chance for the story, because they wouldn't use it without photos. But I thought maybe there was good luck in it for me. I had been unaware the road was in such dire condition. Every one of the people who came into the cabin, except for the three women, said there were cars off the road all along the canyon. The highway patrolman said he expected a busy day. I would have left the cabin late enough to have to rush, and even though I would have known almost at once how slippery the road was, almost at once might also have been too late.

It's not just that one can easily slide into the river (for much of the canyon there is space for only the river and the road), but the big semis that come roaring by between Bozeman and West Yellowstone, as if it were a six-lane interstate instead of a two-lane mountain road, are quite apt to drive down the middle of the road, in bad weather especially. If you skid, and a truck happens to be coming at that moment from either direction, you'd be lucky to get into the river. Two weeks earlier one of the semis even went in, with such force that the cab was crushed like an accordion.

So I felt the women had kept me safe.

Hank and Lonny went to watch the wrecker pull the car out of the river. It had gone in backside first and seemed to be in reasonable shape when it came out. The men drove down to the garage to have a look at it from underneath.

The women were calm now, able to focus on the miracle that none of them had been hurt. "I wonder how they get the water out," Donna said.

At two-thirty Hank came back and announced the car was all right. They had drained the transmission, put in new oil and fixed the trunk, which had jammed open. They all left then.

I folded a couple of blankets they had used and went into the little bedroom off the main room to put them away. There, neatly placed at the foot of the bed, was a five-dollar bill. I cried when I saw it. People in Montana had been wonderful to me since I arrived, and I had been glad to have some way to pay that back. Besides, the feeling that those women had saved me from an even worse accident was powerful. It seemed to me that I owed *them*. They were not rich and they had been scared to death and they might have died, because people do die on that road and in that river. In early winter the icy road had caused a skidding collision between a laundry truck and a woman driving a Subaru. The woman was killed. She was my age. According to the paper her birthday was three days after mine. Taurus. I had driven my Subaru into town that day. The accident happened half an hour after I had passed that spot.

I was certain it had been Donna who had left the money. She was the only one carrying a purse. While dealing with thoughts basic to one's own precious, fragile existence, and coping with the aftermath— when the real terror sets in—of plunging in a car into a fast and winter river, Donna had been concerned about putting me out. It is miraculous here, how much neighbors and strangers matter.

Two weeks later a postcard came from Donna in California. "We had a good trip out," she wrote. "We're having a wonderful time."

The Shrink

The psychologist's office is in the Medical Arts Center on North Willson in Bozeman. There's plenty of parking. Inside, long corridors are lined with doctors of all sorts: eye doctors, ear, nose and throat specialists, cardiologists, internists, radiologists, orthopedists—every specialty known to Montana is present. The corridors are tidy, and the building itself is not actually depressing. It does not have a medicinal smell. You are not subjected to people's pain. The back windows, the ones on the stairwells, look out over the Bridger Range— steep, high, bare peaks that form a spectacular chain squeezed upward between broad valleys and standing like a guard to the north of town.

The office is on the third floor. This seems to be the

psychological floor. Rather, this is where the few psychologists are located. There probably aren't enough of them in Bozeman to fill a whole floor. In the waiting room there are copies of *Natural History, Psychology Today* and *Life*. I stole an issue of *Natural History* because it had a photo of mountain goats on the front of it. I have a passion for mountain goats. Later, when I told someone I'd stolen the magazine, they suggested I might just have asked for it. That never occurred to me.

My first session was spent explaining my distrust of psychologists, based on earlier experiences with several of them, two of them mine, two my husband's. I had come, nevertheless, because I felt driven to the brink—of an abyss, of madness, perhaps of sanity, in any case of impenetrable and unbearable sorrow. I had become willing to risk a situation of distrust in order to find a way out of pain that struck me as both unending and absurd. I had recently been reading a Hesse essay in which he wrote about fully entering one's own pain. Although I understood what I read, and somewhere agreed, I wanted out. Or, barring that, at least a way to use the pain, by which, perhaps, I meant I wanted in. Either way, I needed help. The psychologist had been recommended by a close friend who said he would not insist on a long-term commitment, but would be available as I needed him.

I felt uncomfortable walking into his office. Superior, of course: I was a New Yorker and taller than he. He wore a brown suit that seemed as if it might have a synthetic in it. His office was not unattractive. It had the usual assortment of wall hangings and handsome innocuous objects that in no way attract, or direct, one's emotions, except for a bronze statue of a drooping Indian on his drooping horse known, in various manifestations, as "The Last Ride." This struck me as highly suggestive, but it had been made by his teenage daughter and had to be displayed. I recall only one chair besides the chair at his desk. Perhaps there were more, but they are not in my memory. Was there a couch? What I remember are clocks. There were clocks everywhere. One on the wall opposite his desk, the hands making their way by battery over a western scene; a tiny one on the door frame of what I think is a closet on that same wall, opposite the chair; one on his desk facing the chair; another on the windowsill next to the chair. Each one of the clocks had a slightly different time except for the wall clock, which had a radically different time. On his desk, within arm's reach of the patient in the chair, was a box of yellow Kleenex. The chair was comfortable.

His middle name was Christ. That's not how it's spelled, but that's what it was.

In my diatribe against psychologists I mentioned to him that I had come because I was beating my head against the same things over and over; that wherever I was, it was the wrong place; that I was so trapped in my struggle I could not find my way back to my life.

Looking at me intensely, actually bent toward me in his looking, he said, "When a trout is pulled out of the water he flounders and flounders against the rocks, and if he struggles long enough he lands up back in the water. Bruised, maybe, but back in the stream."

I liked that. I liked the image. I liked it that he had used an image from nature. I left soon afterward, having overstayed my allotted time, but feeling good. I wasn't sure that I thought he was smart enough for me, but he had finished the session with an image guaranteed to draw me back. A few days later I called to make another appointment. I would not set up a regular schedule, wanting neither to be tied to one, nor to make the hour's drive into town without really feeling like a trip to town. That's what I told myself. In fact, I wanted this to be entirely on my terms. I did not want him to expect anything of me. I already saw how excited he was by me, how interesting he found me. This reinforced my feeling that he was not bright enough for me. But I had liked the image. And I had had no one to talk to for so long.

By the next session I had read, fascinated, a piece in the *New Yorker* about the therapist Geoffrey Masson. I entered his office wanting to discuss the article. Had he read it? What did he think of it? *Why* hadn't he read it? It would be necessary for him to read it so we could talk. His not having read it struck me as a sign of intellectual laziness. Why wasn't he reading everything that was written about his field?

I continued seeing him throughout the winter, every two or three weeks, calling for an appointment as I felt the necessity for it. I enjoyed having a specific place to go at a specific time on those days I went into town. I liked the drive to the Medical Arts Center. I liked parking in one of the parking lots connected to it. I actually liked entering the building. I continued to feel superior to the building and its inhabitants, both doctors and patients. First of all, there was nothing physically wrong with me. Second of all, I was a New Yorker.

Sometimes as I climbed the stairs to the third floor and looked out over the Bridger Range, I longed for it to belong to me, for Montana to belong to me. Sometimes I felt I did belong here, that this was, indeed, mine. In those moments I forgot I was a New Yorker. In those moments I became a Montanan. I was at home, climbing stairs in a building I knew, on a street I knew, in a town I knew, in a valley that I claimed. In those moments I did not feel superior until I entered the office and saw him there, greeting me somehow awkwardly in his brown suit. Once I wanted to cry, but managed to keep it back, believing my tears would give him some sort of superiority over me. Usually I left the office feeling better, as if I had understood something new, not necessarily because of anything he had said. But twice I left feeling wretched, and angry he hadn't changed that, knowing as he did that I had an hour's drive—a dangerous time to feel despair—before having to enter, alone, my empty cabin.

Finally, the necessity of working intensely on the book I was writing, combined with the fact that the ski season was in full swing, made me cancel all trips to town. "I won't come again until the ski season is over," I said. "Time off from the book is only to ski."

By late April I was working on the book every waking hour. Its due date was the end of June. I became increasingly aware that, once it was finished, I would be returning to New York. I did not want to go to New York and could not imagine how I would actually get myself there. The act of getting into the car and driving across America seemed out of the question, even though I knew I had no choice. There was unfinished business in New York. It had to be done, but I could not face doing it.

At the same time, the friend who had recommended the psychologist in the first place was, herself, in despair. Badly wanting to adopt a child, she had been callously dealt with by the social worker with whom she was dealing; to whom she had looked as the last of all possible avenues. The psychologist listened to her, then charted out an entirely practical course of action. She left his office with a sense that what she wanted was neither absurd nor impossible, and that she was in no way unfit, as the social worker had so determinedly tried to impart to her.

Then I understood that he could get me to New York, and I went to see him. I felt the comfort of returning to a place I knew. People with appointments were actual people. They must exist if they had appointments. When I climbed the stairs, the Bridger Range was still there, still covered with snow, although there was a sense of spring in town. I was pleased that I would be able to present him with a purely practical problem: How was I to get myself to New York?

"The thing is," I said, "I don't want to pass my husband on the street. I don't want to risk passing him with someone else on the street."

"But you have a choice," the psychologist said. "You are not at his mercy. You can pass and say hello, or pass and not say hello. You can look at him or away. You can walk into a doorway or cross the street. You can smile or not. How you act is entirely up to you. You have choices."

"Between the guillotine and a firing squad."

"Choices, nonetheless. You are in charge."

When it was time to leave, he asked me if I wanted to make a series of appointments. I was reluctant.

"You can cancel if you find you can't keep one," he said.

I felt it was a kind of control over me. I also felt I needed to make the appointments. "You're sure I can cancel?"

"Of course."

It allowed me to set up a schedule.

It was the second time he had given me something to use. I could make choices. I could struggle long enough to get back into the stream. At the next session I asked if I could see the notes he had been taking. He seemed taken aback.

"You're making notes about me, right?" I asked.

"Yes, but only so I can keep things in mind."

"But they're about me. Doctors are forever making notes they will not show their patients. As if doctors

84

were entitled to some secret view of patients. As if what the doctors saw about the patient would be dangerous to the patient. The patient is not to be trusted with his self. It's part of what's wrong with this. These notes are about me. Therefore they belong to me."

"But they're not very interesting," he said. "They're just reminders for me."

"I'm not very interesting?"

"My notes aren't."

"I'm not interested in their literary merit. I just want access to what is mine. The fact that you won't let me see them leads me to believe there's something about me you're keeping from me. Otherwise, why not? Why shouldn't I know what seems of importance to you?"

He paused. "It's just that . . . I didn't want you to think I was a bozo."

Bozo. The local word for someone from Bozeman. A logical word, given the name of the town. But synonymous with hick, hillbilly.

My heart went out to him. He saw me feeling superior. I existed in another world. It was a world not foreign to him, although he saw I did not include him in it. That he had been willing to say it affected me. Growing up in a place so little known to the rest of the world that most people don't even know it exists, could easily cause anyone to feel an insecurity outside of it. Most of us are like that. We can comprehend the world, but not feel part of it. We move through the world, always a little removed from it. Almost always. Unless we are lucky enough to come home.

Bozo. A clown in a world of high-wire aerialists and bareback riders. The horses are white and prance high. The aerialists swing daringly from trapezes, twirling through air held still by the breathless hush of an audience that cannot believe the trick can be done, the final turn achieved, the flyer caught. The audience is always prepared for the crash. The trick seems impossible, the risk unforgivable, the confidence and skill unfathomable, the dream an illusion of flying. The aerialist wears a white costume with silver, glittering spangles. In triumph, he grandly raises one arm, a salute that takes in heaven. Afterward, Bozo comes in to perform his act in the sawdust of the ring, his face painted for the sadness that makes people laugh. It is the relief of not having to fly. Anymore. Bozo, arbiter of our sorrow. The one who gets pushed around. Hillbilly. Hick. The one who isn't good enough to glitter. It was not the psychologist, not Christ, who was Bozo.

Bighorn Sheep

T he fifteenth of April was brilliantly clear and warm. Although there was still plenty of snow at the ski area and on the north- and west-facing slopes, the hills opposite the cabin were brown, bared by days of warm sun. I had been wanting to walk them ever since they began emerging from their winter cover.

Starting out at the Deer Creek Trailhead, a couple of miles down the road from my cabin, I climbed, slowly, the snow-free slopes that front the canyon road. The trail itself, winding along the creek and back behind the slopes I could see, into the Spanish Peaks, lay still buried. Even along my route an occasional deep patch of old snow, packed as it was from so much sun and melting, snared my foot. The newly released scent of sagebrush was strong, and the air swelled with its smell and the scent of pine. Then the wild, musky odor of bighorn sheep swept over the hillside. It came rolling down, like an avalanche. The sky was cloudless. To the north, the peaks of the Gallatin Range across the canyon were bright with snow that became darkly treed as the range ran south toward me and, farther south, to Yellowstone. Winter lasts longer on that side of the canyon.

A bighorn sheep grazed the next ridge over, tan against the deep blue sky. She was simply there, on top of the ridge. The world consisted of only this: the sheep, the sloping brown earth, the deep blue sky. I climbed higher than the sheep. Suddenly, a small herd of bighorns appeared out of the draw between the sheep's ridge and the next one over. They ran up the sloping meadow of that far one, then disappeared over the edge.

The solitary sheep ignored them. She walked slowly up the ridge, sensed me, stopped, looked toward me, locked eyes with me, stood absolutely still, started again, slowly, upward, stopped. Her head was straight forward now. She was no longer looking at me. She seemed to be listening. For what? A move from me? A sound of danger? She repeated this process of walking, stopping, listening several times until she disappeared over the top of the ridge. It seemed deliberate, as if she wanted to leave, but didn't want to let on she was in a rush.

I stood about twenty feet below the top, at the edge of the snow line, probably about two miles from the road. A sun-warmed rock a few feet away seemed the perfect spot for lunch.

I spent an hour or so on the rock. During this time nothing happened. There was no wind. No clouds appeared. The snow did not visibly melt. Spring did not come farther up the mountain but seemed to hang where it was, suspended, held in the soft, light promise of the noon. It was too early in the Montana year for spring, but rather than abandon its first, tentative moments, it lay motionless, a gentle breath held long enough to give us—the bighorn sheep and me and the earth—the memory and promise of spring, a gift to carry with us through the blizzards that still lay ahead.

By mid-April it is possible to be tired of winter. Even those who welcome the purity and silence of winter are ready for spring by then. But you cannot rush spring in Montana. You cannot invent seasons, order time around, insist on calendars made by man. You go through winter, and one day spring comes. It begins subtly, as the snow draws back in the valley and the first glacier lilies appear at its edges. Suddenly a green appears that you had not remembered. The edge of the forest seems greener than it had before, as if this particular spring was newer than spring had ever been. It eases up the mountains until, by mid-July, all the snow that's going has gone.

On my walk down the mountain I saw the herd on their far meadow. The solitary sheep stood almost where she had stood earlier. Why was she alone? We looked at one another longer this time. She did not move. It was up to me to make a move. It was I, after all, who had entered her world. Either I must be prepared to stay forever as a bighorn sheep, or make a move to leave, as an invader. I turned and walked slowly down, occasionally stopping, turning to look back. Each time I looked, she was still there. She had not moved. She was watching me.

Near the bottom a man came along the path paralleling the creek. "Did you see any lion tracks up there?" he asked.

I had seen no tracks. The man and I talked a few moments. As we stood talking, I noticed three little, yellow sage buttercups above him on the side of a brown hill. Each one was quite far from the others.

"Are you ready for spring?" I asked.

He shrugged. He told me he had wintered as the caretaker of a private property on the Deer Creek Road. "I'll be leaving for Alaska soon," he said.

The Opera Season in Bozeman

T he Bozeman Opera
season is two nights in May. Lead singers, sets and
costumes are imported from the Metropolitan Opera
in New York, while the chorus, and some of the smaller
parts, fall to local singers who rehearse the year's
opera for months. Performances are held in the auditorium of the Willson School on Main Street, the stage
used by many of the touring companies that pass
through Bozeman. I had attended a fairly bad modern
dance concert at the Willson School in the fall, after
which I decided the level of cultural events in town did
not warrant the hour's drive through the canyon. But
I had promised a neighbor I would go with her to this
year's production, *Madame Butterfly*. The event, and
the music, were important to her. Excited about it

months in advance, she ordered tickets the moment the dates were announced. The opera was well promoted on Bozeman radio. I went, expecting it would be awful, but ready to exercise my duty as a friend.

We arrived early, opened the school doors . . . and stepped across a boundary. The line was an absolute one, defined by the door jamb. On one side were the steps of the Willson School on Main Street, America; on the other a rare and fragrant oriental garden. Fuchsia, overflowing, overgrowing, sensual and flamboyant, hung from the ceiling and poured over plant stands in the entranceway lobby, the flowers exploding out of their pots like fireworks, some innocently pink and white; some entirely, ripely pink; some pink and an amazing deep purple, deeper than understanding, as deep as sorrow. Mustard-brown Japanese paper parasols lay opened in a semicircle behind the fuchsia. A pink carpet led from the entranceway through this garden to the auditorium doors.

Did we speak in whispers . . . ?

Just before the curtain, the audience settled and expectant, a member of the Opera Society's board—a local nursery operator whose radio commercials feature his own voice providing helpful hints for tending one's lawn—strode onto the stage, greeted his friends, neighbors and customers, which no doubt included most of the audience, and announced that the promised Pablo Elvira would not appear.

Elvira, who is at home in Bozeman with his wife and family when he is not singing elsewhere, is the Star of Bozeman. I find it interesting that the Star of Bozeman is an opera singer rather than a world champion rodeo cowboy. He had been detained in San Francisco by something important, but had sent a telegram in which he apologized profusely to us, assuring us he loved and missed us and would see us next year in *La Traviata*. After the telegram was read, his wife, seated toward the front of the auditorium, on the left, waved to us.

The curtain opened. Ferns, and more pots of fuchsia, had been incorporated into the set—a garden, a gentle, still place overlooking the sea. The chorus entered dressed in kimonos so delicate and exquisite that it was as if a seawave of beauty had washed over the audience, pulling it into a world of some rare and fragile beauty that was both unattainable and engulfing. It happened so quickly. It was utterly complete. I could not keep from crying.

I had not seen *Butterfly* since I was a child and, I suppose because it is so popular, have always thought of it as slight.

Childhood had not prepared me for that music. Nor

for Butterfly herself.

The first act was not badly sung, appealing enough that it allowed the audience a pleasant sociability during intermission. "It's too bad Pablo couldn't be here," people said to one another. "But his replacement is doing a good job, don't you think? " other people would reply, after which conversation turned to the sets, the flowers, the costumes that had had to be flown out from New York because they were too fragile to travel by truck. Then they returned to their seats for the second act.

It hit from the beginning. Before us the world wavered between despair and hope, despair and belief, all the extremes of the human soul contained in Butterfly as she stands, waiting, at the door, her back to the audience, her arms up, bent at the elbows, hands pressed against the door, the red silk of her robe flowing, folding down from her shoulders in such a way that the folds hold expectation, hope, belief. The moment, the posture, the life is so excruciating, so still, so full of silence, so doomed and so beautiful, it can hardly be borne. Her death is a relief, a release from hope as much as from despair.

At the end I felt the tears in the eyes of the audience—that instant that is an eternity before the applause; that instant in which the audience cannot act.

Then, a standing ovation. Five minutes later, as the audience began the walk up the aisles to the exit, before I could yet move, I saw the faces with their tears held inside, so that people hardly even smiled at people they knew.

The performance was at six o'clock. When we left the theater, the sky lay like molten gold over the mountains, lay in strips of white and light gold and heavy, heavy gold. We stood on the school steps and did not speak.

Polar John's Bar

Polaris, Montana, can be reached from the north via thirty miles of dirt road, or from the south on twenty-nine miles of paved road from Dillon, the Big Hole Valley's major town (population: 3,976), then six miles of dirt road. There are three buildings in Polaris: a large log structure that houses the post office, the general store and an apartment; a small log cabin; and a still smaller, white frame building that is Polar John's Bar. Polar John lives over the post office. His brother-in-law lives in the cabin. If the bar is closed and you want a beer, you knock on Polar John's door and he comes down and opens the bar.

In 1981 the bar was the focus of a major conflict between the state health authorities and the people of Polaris and surrounding communities, including Dillon. The health department wanted to close Polar John's on the grounds that its plumbing was inadequate, equipped as it was with only one outhouse when separate facilities for men and women are required in public places, and with no hot water to wash the glasses. On May 3, 1981, a march to save Polar John's john was held.

Hundreds marched.

The result of this action was that the local citizens dug, and built, a second outhouse. Each outhouse has an equally good view of the valley. The health department then agreed that Polar John could use plastic, disposable glasses in the bar. Since most Montanans drink beer out of a can anyway, he can keep his overhead low.

The bar is a simple, square room containing an oilcloth-covered round table in one corner, with benches on two sides of it and a couple of ice cream chairs in front of it. A few wooden chairs, a stool and a rocker line up against two walls. There is a pot-bellied stove near the front door and an old oak bar with a brass rail. The bar comes from Bannack, Montana's first territorial capital and site, in 1863, of Montana's first gold rush. Two years of cold-blooded violence at the hands of a band of road agents, ably led by the Bannack sheriff, made Bannack one of the roughest towns in the West. When the local citizenry finally tired of being robbed and murdered so often, they formed a vigilante committee, pinning its secret sign, "3-7-77," on hanged bandits. *All* bandits were hanged. The vigilantes managed to capture the entire gang. And then some. Those numbers, 3-7-77, appear today on road signs in southwest Montana and on shoulder patches of the Montana State Police throughout the state. No one can explain what they mean.

Five of us had spent several days backpacking in the West Pioneer Range. The paths we walked were far gentler than the miles of dirt road and one-lane, rock-strewn pass we had driven over to reach the bar. Because the lakes in the West Pioneers are heavily used, we had been boiling the water we drank. Aside from the fact that boiled water tastes awful, it is a pain in the neck to boil enough to drink on a hot Montana day, so we drank less than our bodies required. By the time we reached the bar we were in serious need of beer.

When we entered Polar John's, a dog was sleeping on the floor, two old cowboys were sitting on wooden chairs drinking beer, Polar John was standing behind the bar and a horse was looking in through the open back door. One of the old cowboys said, "Howdy."

Howdy is an interesting word. In my years of backpacking and hiking, every man I have ever passed in wilderness anywhere in America, even in Harriman Park, forty minutes from New York City, has greeted me with "howdy." These men may be stockbrokers or physicians or engineers who dress in suits and ties on weekdays and greet people with "good morning" or "how are you?," but no sooner do they get into the forest or the mountains than they say, "howdy."

No woman I have ever encountered in the wilderness has greeted me with "howdy."

All three men watched us arrange ourselves on bar stools, take in the bar, try not to appear too curious about them, open our beer. The man who had greeted us turned out to be Polar John's brother-in-law, seventy-seven-year-old Walt Melcher, who quickly connected with one of our group, sixty-six-year-old Bill Barnes, a farmer from the Montana plains. Born in the Big Belt Mountains that edge the plains, Bill had now retired to Great Falls.

He had also just returned from a kayak trip of several weeks in Alaska. His keen interest in everything on earth kept him from any semblance of shyness. Of us all, he was the only one to openly explore his environment in the bar. He began a conversation with Polar John. I suspect it may have been the only conversation Polar John has ever had.

Turning square to him, Bill said, "You've been here quite a while, haven't you?"

A few minutes passed. Finally Polar John said, "Yeah." Then he resumed the silence he'd been moved out of by so direct a question.

"He was born here in nineteen-ten," Walt offered. Watching us seemed to amuse him. His eyes laughed. Clearly there was nothing shy about him, either.

Polar John stood behind the bar, tall and slender, straight as a young man. He continued saying nothing.

"I was born in nineteen-eighteen," Bill said.

"You're lucky to be here," Walt said.

"Yeah, that's true," Bill agreed.

"You probably had a pretty good life," the old cowboy added.

"Yeah, that's probably true too," Bill said.

When he realized there would be a conversation, the silent cowboy got up from his chair as if he didn't want to be in the way of it and ambled over to the end of the bar where he joined Polar John in saying nothing. He stood, rolling a cigarette and watching the two old men of the land talk. It was obvious that if it were not for Walt, there never would be a conversation in Polaris.

They had the land in common, the farmer and the cowboy, and although neither of them worked it anymore, it had formed their tenacity and their humor. They found each other the way children discover one another in a gathering of adults, or the way people of the same nationality find one another on foreign soil.

The dog lifted his head. Walt moved to the wooden stool, raised his leg straight out in front of him. The dog jumped over it several times.

"Usually he does this for potato chips," Walt said.

"Does he work cattle?" Bill asked.

"Well, he's awful good when they're well cooked," Walt said.

It was seven forty-five. The light was fading. Walt said, "You should see the Big Hole Valley while you're here."

"I always meant to," Bill said, "but I think I picked the wrong time. I'm supposed to be in Great Falls by eight."

It is a three-hour drive from Polar John's Bar to Great Falls, out there at the edge of the prairie where the great falls of the Missouri gave birth to the town. There are five falls in a ten-mile stretch of river, the highest of which is the farthest upstream and the one which Meriwether Lewis called the Great Falls in his first view of them:

... The grandest sight I ever beheld ... the irregular and somewhat projecting rocks below receives the water in it's passage down and brakes it into a perfect white foam which assumes a thousand forms in a moment sometimes flying up in jets of sparkling foam to the hight of fifteen or twenty feet and are scarcely formed before large roling bodies of the same beaten and foaming water is thrown over and conceals them.

The falls now have been harnessed to provide electrical power.

"Well, there's a jet that flies over ... ," Walt offered as a way to get Bill home on schedule.

The other cowboy spoke for the first time. "Montana is a goddamn big state," he said.

I bought a bag of potato chips for the dog. He jumped back and forth over my leg which I held increasingly higher. Each time he ate his potato chip before jumping back. When the bag of potato chips was empty, he lay down and went to sleep. At eight-fifteen Bill rose from his chair, saying, "I've got to see Polar John's john, then I'm going to Great Falls."

Walt said, "There's a million acres out there. You can use every one of 'em."

At the back door, Bill looked out on the million

acres, then turned and asked, "Where is it?"

Walt followed him out, saying, to us or to himself, "I better go show him. Awful hard to hit that little hole."

Now that everyone who talked had left the bar, the bar was silent again. A second horse walked by the back door.

Tyrol

There are other places to live besides Montana. Similar places. Wyoming. Alaska. Places that are big. That have space in them. Places where wildness is a fact of life. Even their names sound wide open, coming off your tongue like a wind rolling off the prairie. *Montana.* I say it as I would the name of a beloved; a magical, sacred word.

There was a time when I said the word *Austria* the same way. Austria was the beginning of high mountains for me, a kind of birth. It is not odd I felt a passion toward it.

I lived in Innsbruck for a while in the sixties. Traveling from there to America to visit my parents, I met the man I married, and I stayed. I hadn't meant to stay, but marriage can interrupt one's life. Now, before deciding permanently on Montana, I wanted to visit Europe, to see, with an eye toward living there again, if I was still as drawn to it as I had been. Europe had been a major fork in the road for me. I wanted to see if I could go back along the road and, this time, take the other fork.

I went first to Scharnitz, a small town not far from the German border, a short train ride from Innsbruck. From here there is easy access into the heart of the Karwendel Mountains. When I first came here, visitors had to walk about five miles up a rutted old wagon road, and the trail that occasionally deviates from it, to reach the Karwendelhaus, a refuge built by the German Alpine Club in 1908. The road was used for transporting supplies from Scharnitz to the hut. That was the first hike I made alone in the Alps, the beginning of a walk more or less from Innsbruck to Salzburg across the mountains.

It had been a stormy day, and I was wet and cold. The wind sapped my strength. I had not known what lay ahead. Nor, in my discomfort, could I remember why I wanted to do this. When, late in the walk, the clouds lifted for a moment to reveal the old stone hut high above me, flush to the edge of the mountain on a narrow ledge, the hut seemed too high, too far away. The mountain continued up behind the hut, its rock and the rock of the hut blending into one another. There was nothing to do but keep going.

I pulled open the heavy door to enter a dark hallway, passing the brightly lit kitchen where women in white coats were cutting and pounding and stirring things. It looked warm and happy. The people had a function. As I took off my wet boots in the hall, the door opened, the wind blasting in behind it. A young man entered. "Were you on top? " he asked when he saw me.

"No, I just came up from Scharnitz," I said.

He must have come down from one summit or another, feeling the adventure of the storm, but when I turned out to be no comrade in it, he removed his boots without saying anything more, took a pair of slippers from the shelf, and disappeared into the guest room at the far end of the hall. I extracted my own slippers from my pack and went into the kitchen to ask about a space to sleep.

It was a long time ago.

Now I walked up the road in hot sun, a new dirt road, prepared for cars. Nobody walks to the hut from Scharnitz anymore. I could have taken a cab, but I wanted to arrive as I had first arrived. Since that first trip I have spent a good deal of time in the hut, so now my first view of it above me was like a view of home, a place that waits for you.

I entered the kitchen to be greeted with hugs by my friends who run the hut: Birgit and her mother, Wilma. They are something of an anomaly in Austria. The alpine huts are maintained by various sections of the Austrian and German alpine clubs, each section hiring its own manager. The Karwendelhaus has seen an altogether rare succession of managers: women, first of all, and then three generations of women in the same family—first Wilma's aunt, then Wilma, and now Birgit. But Birgit has no daughter and, when she leaves, a chain remarkable in Austria will be broken.

When I first came, Birgit's father had been there too. He was an old man then, and ill. He sat quietly at the table, his drawn face giving no clue to the robust man he had been. One winter during the war he had hidden several Jews in the hut, skiing up to bring them food and supplies. There was an SS garrison in Scharnitz, but he had rightly guessed that no soldiers would follow him up the mountain in the Tyrolean winter. If he was stopped, he would say he had to check on the hut. Caught, he would have been shot.

Now her father was dead and Birgit was married and the sun was hot. Now I did not have to ask awkwardly, in a German I was not sure would work, about a place to sleep. Now Birgit gave me a special room. On that first trip I was an outsider. Then the guest room was filled with groups of hikers singing and drinking and waiting out the weather. Only I was alone. This time I never even entered the guest room, but, when I was not out walking in the mountains, sat at the family table in the kitchen or in a beautiful little room the family used—its walls and ceiling of carved wood. Birgit and Wilma plied me with food, the Tyrolean specialties at which they are masters, and too much of the best of pastries. They could not do enough. I felt protected, utterly safe.

The first morning, I hiked the switchback trail up the Hochalmkreuz, the peak above the hut. The path is wide and almost smooth. From the summit I looked out across the Karwendel Range: jagged, high, bare peaks with long slides of gray scree stretching down from them; limestone walls; the harsh, unyielding landscape I had loved instantly. I had learned these mountains fairly well. Seeing them as fiercely beautiful, I had wanted them forever.

But now, after spending considerable time in the Rockies, I was aware that, outside of the intrinsic challenge mountains offer, and the possibilities of weather, here, in the Alps, there was nothing wild around me:

no cougars, no bears, no nighttime song of coyotes. There were chamois, marmots, storms, wildflowers, but nothing demanding the wariness that is a matter of course in the Rockies. In good weather I could walk here in a dream—although it is always necessary to keep an eye out for the edge of a cliff or the suddenness of a rock avalanche. So often in Montana's mountains I had longed for the Alps—for a moment to let down my guard, for a moment to stop thinking about bears, about coming between a moose and her calf, about inadvertently stumbling on a lion's cache. Yet it was precisely that that I now missed—the need to be alert that I craved, the wariness that made of me something wild. Kin to all the wild things. Years before, on a walk in another Tyrolean range, I had passed a bronze plaque nailed to a boulder. "The last bear in Tyrol was shot on this spot," the plaque said. I could never figure out whether the proclamation had been made in triumph or in sorrow.

On the way down the Hochalmkreuz, I encountered a group of Germans dressed in knickers, checked shirts, Tyrolean hats. The *de rigeur* alpine hiking outfit. I had once dressed like that. It was what one wore in the Alps. I had liked the way it looked. It had seemed functional. Now it struck me as silly. The whole group of them struck me as silly. I hurried down the mountain as, singing a hiking song, they continued up. The kitchen was not silly. Birgit and Wilma were not silly.

After lunch I intended to climb another mountain, one a bit farther from the hut. But Wilma said to me, "You must rest." She didn't say *why* I must rest, but she said it so authoritatively that I thought she must be right. Maybe this was the time I was to recover from my marriage. Europeans allow themselves luxuries Americans do not. Rest. Yes. I suddenly felt that I had come for a cure. Europeans are always going off to take a cure. My body might be eager to climb a mountain, but my spirit was glad to lie in the sun and sip tea. Wilma is a wise woman.

She arranged a chaise for me behind the hut, on the small plot of grass before the land rises almost vertically up the mountain. I lay in the sun and wrote letters. After all this time since my marriage had ended, someone, at last, had recognized that I was tired.

Rain came the next day, presenting a kind of wildness, a solitude for sure, since no one else would go out on such a day. I crossed the high meadow below the hut to follow a path winding along the side of the mountains to the north. I think I crossed the border into Germany somewhere along the route. Smuggling here would be no big deal, if one could decide what to smuggle, then get it into either Austria or Germany in the first place, depending on which country one wanted to smuggle it *from*. That, of course, would be the trick. The trail came out onto a scree slope where I saw two chamois. The chamois and the stone and the sky were all the same color.

The rain turned to snow the following day. I did not leave the hut for the several days it continued, until, restless, I went down to Innsbruck where I stayed in Wilma's apartment. When she is not in the Karwendelhaus, she lives in a high-ceilinged, spacious, rambling space in a pre-war building next door to Emperor Maximilian I's arsenal and not far from the Sill River. A few blocks away, the Sill enters the Inn, the broad green river that has come down from Switzerland to form the Inn Valley and given its name to the city. *Innsbruck.* Bridge over the Inn. From the river you look north to the Karwendel Range, rising like some wall of the gods at the edge of the city.

Mornings I ran along the Sill, the only person running. Daily I encountered an elderly woman walking a wire-haired terrier. She looked at me sternly. No one I passed said good morning. One day I stopped to talk to the dog. I had had a wire-hair for sixteen years. The dog died the year before my husband left. After I mentioned that to the woman—about the dog, not my husband—she always greeted me smilingly. Once she invited me to her house. Running was not acceptable, but owning a wire-haired terrier was. More and more I saw how tradition here dictates what is acceptable. This world is a narrow one. I had not felt this when I lived here, when I had been looking for definitions, boundaries, the kind of tradition that would provide me with an external form so I could stop struggling with everything at once, that would allow me to let go of having to make all my own rules as I went along.

Afternoons I wandered the streets of Innsbruck, trying to remember why it was I had come. The streets were completely familiar to me, yet I could not remember how I had felt on them when I had lived here. I was different. I no longer required definitions. The streets were the same.

Living in a language other than my own had seemed a freedom when I lived in Innsbruck. To some extent it still does. In another language you are freed of the responsibility that comes with belonging to a place. Forever a stranger, you are forever free. But now I saw another side to that. Even if you understand a language well, there remains a place you can never go; some subtle place in understanding that exists only in your mother tongue. Our language forms the way we think. You can share the words of another language with those who speak it, but to share what language only suggests, you need someone whose native tongue is yours. When I lived in Innsbruck, I was content in German; I stayed away from Americans. Now I sometimes longed to have a cup of coffee with an American, to speak a language that was mine.

Kilometer Zero

I went to Paris to speak English. Taking the night train from Innsbruck, I arrived just before dawn, the hour one ought to arrive. Not only is it actually possible to find a cab then, but the city, empty, is entirely yours. There is no one on the boulevards. Shrouded in slight mists, the globe lamps lining the bridges shed light on no passerby. Only buildings emerge from the night, gray against the gray-mauve sky, monuments to a life that was there yesterday and will come again today.

My cab crossed the Seine at the Ile de la Cité, passed the still-dark Palace of Justice, arrived in Montparnasse as the sky lightened to a soft gray, pearl gray, dove gray; the Paris gray that wraps you, caresses you, teaches you about color things you never imagined.

As we turned a corner onto the little street where Eric lives, Eric came running down it toward us. "I picked up croissants," he said as he opened the cab door. It had been years since I had seen him, but he had always known what really mattered.

Eric is an American who has lived in Europe for over twenty years, running a consulting business nobody but he can understand. It was he who had developed the proposed public transit system for Montana, years before Montana ever occurred to me. He is an American with whom I could have a cup of coffee.

People have gone to Paris for less.

Actually, Paris had been on my agenda all along. Part of making a decision about Montana involved deciding whether I was ready to leave large cities behind. New York was out of the question. My husband lived there. I would not live there anymore. But Paris possesses a vitality similar to New York's and is more civilized, besides. I am fond of civilization. Civilization and wildness. It's the middle I can't bear. The suburbs. The median. The mean. The moderate, careful, practical place that allows you to get through life with a minimum of hassle. It's not that I like hassle. It's just that I loathe its opposite. Austria, showing me what I missed in Montana, had shown its position in that middle place. But I was not yet ready to leave Europe, and I could not choose Montana without giving Paris a shot.

What I wanted from Eric was a little time in my native tongue without having to resort to my native land. Then too, Paris itself seems a kind of monument to English. Joyce, Hemingway, Stein, Fitzgerald, Eliot, Sylvia Beach's bookstore—Shakespeare & Co.—what better place to be when one is hungry for English? *They* had all taken their hunger for English to Paris. In Paris, City of the World, the writer in English has the luxury of being both a foreigner and at home.

The problem I now encountered with this state of being, which had been one so important to me, was the recent sense of my own country that had interposed itself in the form of Montana. This stood to become either a passion that would direct the rest of my life or an inconvenience with which I would have to deal. I expected Paris would make clearer which— passion or inconvenience.

Eric said he understood my need to speak English, but that it would be necessary for me to learn French. "You cannot consider living in a place if you cannot speak the language," he said, as he trundled me off to the Alliance Française. In his own, flawless French, he convinced them to let me in, although classes started that same day and registration was closed.

There were a couple of Americans in the class, plus a Swede, a German, a Korean, a Pakistani, an Iraqi, an Iranian, a Japanese, a Peruvian. The Iraqi, the Iranian and the Pakistani always sat together. The class, conducted entirely in French, met four hours a day. French was supposed to be our only common language. This did not keep most of the class from resorting to English when there was a problem in French, since it was hard to accept a language as common without knowing a word of it. Only the Korean had absolutely no English. She didn't seem to be getting much French either.

During the daily half-hour break, all the classes swarmed down the wide marble stairs to the coffee machine, or outside into the courtyard, where one could see that most of the students were Middle Easterners. Eric called them terrorists, although I doubt they all were.

Every morning before school I went for a run in the Luxembourg Gardens. I ran on broad, soft paths, past perfect lawns and precise flower beds, past statues that seemed to suddenly appear from behind a tree as if play came naturally to them, past the grave delight of the fountain of the Medicis. No one ever walks on the lawns. Or sits on them. People sit on benches along the paths. There is no graffiti on the benches. Everywhere you look is something beautiful, harmonious, artful, orderly, imposing, regal, beguiling, historic, reassuring. Reassuring, knowing that beauty endures, surviving revolution, wars and fashion. Now, instead of kings strolling in the gardens, there are students from the Sorbonne and the University of Paris and all the other schools in the neighborhood, but this constitutes little change because students and kings both possess an autonomy largely unavailable to other people. But it's hard to imagine a king buying a crêpe from the vendor in the gardens, then sitting on a bench to eat it while contemplating existentialism and hoping the crêpe won't drip on his pants. Existentialism probably isn't what Parisian students contemplate anymore, but I doubt French kings ever did. I'm sure Marie de Medicis, for whom the gardens and adjoining palace were built in 1615, never did.

Marie—consort of Henry IV, then regent for her son the dauphin—and I have the same birthday, although she is almost four hundred years older than I am. In spite of the difference in our age and the immensity of her political ineptitude, with which I'd as soon not identify, our birthday provides me a sort of empathy with her. It was probably not entirely her fault she was such a screwup. Taurus, which she was, may simply be too ruled by emotion to be making major political decisions, and basically too honest for intrigue. It was just her bad luck to be born into an age when intrigue was practically a social obligation.

Most of the runners in the Luxembourg Gardens are men. None say hello as they pass, as do runners in New York. The whole atmosphere is so entirely different that I understood, suddenly, how *alike* New York and Montana are. In the Luxembourg Gardens there is none of the disorder of Riverside Park, where people and dogs are everywhere on the grass, the walks, the walls; where gardens defy precision as if color could never be contained, the flowers as rambunctious as the Frisbee players, jugglers, bicyclists, dogs and assorted madmen, all of whom are stopped from spilling over into the rest of America only by the Hudson. The Hudson is a good river. Coming down to New York from the mountains, it beckons you into the hinterlands, luring you to follow the water to its source. It demands exploration, adventure, as any proper river does, while the perfection of the long pool extending from the Medicis' fountain invites reverie. The two parks, therefore, offer a vast difference in outlook. Even if one compares the Hudson to the

Seine, there is a difference. The Seine, bisecting the city, forms its heart; the Hudson, separating the city from the mainland, forms its boundary. Heart and boundary are opposites. Still, Paris remains for me the only city in the world comparable in spirit and energy to New York. Paris is more beautiful than New York, or possibly anywhere, but New York, more flawed, rawer, is less confining, even if it is an island. I had always thought of New York as a different country from the rest of America, but in Paris I understood how completely American it is.

After class I wandered around Paris, walking without any particular aim, going where the streets led, often finding myself a little lost when I tried to return home. Getting lost was nice, since it always led me somewhere new, but the times I did not get lost allowed me to feel as if I had begun to know Paris.

I spent hours in the Orangerie and the Jeu de Paume. Crossing the Tuileries, from the Louvre to the Place de la Concorde to reach the two little museums, I crossed centuries of French history. It didn't really matter if I couldn't keep most of it straight. What mattered was that it was alive. In Montana, too, I had felt the nearness of history. Montana's history is not very old, but it is utterly present. What mattered in the museums seemed to be not so much the paintings at which I looked but being surrounded by them. Cézanne and Monet and Matisse were present, not simply as paintings mounted on a wall but as painters in their own place. (Renoir was there too, but I have always loathed Renoir. Paris does not change this.)

One Sunday morning I took the train to Giverny, Monet's home for the second half of his life. How many hours of my own life had I spent in New York's Museum of Modern Art surrounded by the water lilies of Giverny, feeling myself completely inside this world of water and light? For years I had imagined that if I could just get to Giverny, I could turn that around and be inside the paintings, become a part of this soft waterscape, drown, I suppose, in a way. Drown to all that was not beauty. I had imagined the paintings and the pool to be alike. The artist had, after all, made both. Yet, as I stood on his Japanese bridge, I felt nowhere near the paintings. This was a separate event. I had entered nature, as I had in Montana. It didn't matter that the nature had been organized by the artist. Although it was too late in the year for the wisteria to be in bloom or, for that matter, most of the flowers, enough lingered to provide some faded sense of Monet's palette. The willows around the pool were golden in a gold October sun. Masses of plants lining the banks and backing away across the path like some gold-green secret drew my eye from the water, until some dancing moment of sun pulled it back again. I had arrived early enough that there were not yet other visitors. For an hour the garden was mine. I felt as if I walked inside a man's dream.

The water lily paintings are larger than life. The thing about the actual pool is that it is not. Its beauty is one the eye can incorporate, the soul can comprehend. One can *see* how it was done—the pool dug to be fed by the Epte River, the bank planted with iris, and peonies, lilacs, wisteria, roses, azaleas, rhododendron, weeping willows, ferns; the water planted with every known variety of water lily. There is a serenity in the photographs of Monet painting in his garden, the garden itself his painting; a sense of knowing this is the right place, although to make it right, Monet had to build it. The important thing is that he recognized it from the beginning. He *knew* the place would be his work.

There were days when I spent hours browsing the shelves of books in Shakespeare & Co.'s labyrinth of creaking rooms, as much for what the bookshop in its present incarnation conjures up of the original as for the pleasure of the books and the connection it provided me with English. Even though I had come to Paris for the English, here, surrounded by the exquisite language of Paris, English hit with a force I had not anticipated. This was no common language I possessed.

The advantage I felt at never having been in the original Shakespeare & Co.—where all those English-speaking, English-writing expatriots of the twenties were so nurtured by Sylvia Beach—was that my fantasy was unhindered. Imagining what I could never have known of Joyce and Hemingway and Eliot, they could as easily have been in this shop as in Sylvia Beach's. This one possessed part of her book collection, so why not the spirit of her shop? It was that one, hers, I entered each time I opened the shop door, although I never entered quite as I *meant* to enter. I *meant* to enter with a flourish, to be a part of it, but instead I eased my way into various corners, remaining silent, watching the familiarity with which other people who came into the shop engaged with present owner George Whitman. It seemed that all other people who came in engaged with him. I probably wouldn't have talked with anyone in the twenties either. The question, of course, is, would they have talked to me?

In Montana there is a restaurant at Chico Hot Springs,

just north of Yellowstone Park, that attracts writers, painters and filmmakers iconoclastic enough to choose a place so far from Paris. Its owner, Mike Art, once told me that sometimes, sitting at a table with Jim Harrison and Tom McGuane and Russell Chatham, he thinks, "These are my friends. This is like being in Paris in the 1920s."

On my way to school each day, I passed Gertrude Stein's apartment on the rue de Fleurus. It was here, after leaving America, that she lived much of her life. I have a postcard that is a photo of her sitting in a high-ceilinged room on a sofa next to her large white poodle. The poodle's name is Pépé. On the wall behind them is a painting of the dog. In New York I saw a musical called *The Making of Americans*. Drawn from her monumental novel, it is about the hard, long, heart-wrenching, hopeful journey from Russia to America; the journey from one life to all the rest of life. It is about being willing to let go of all that is familiar and that you love because it is yours, in order to embrace all that is strange so that you can come to that place you have always been going. It is about heading west to a new land. It is about heading west to a new life.

The book itself requires the reader to let go of all that is familiar; to embrace a strangeness in language in order to come to a place both completely new and somehow always known.

Did Stein, an American, have to leave America to go there so completely? Must one be a stranger in order to have a home? Is home the place that is left or the place at which one arrives? Why, after the initial uprooting, does permanence become forever so brief?

Upstairs in Shakespeare & Co., George Whitman provides a place to stay for writers working on fiction. One late afternoon I was invited to have a look. A steep, narrow, awkward stairway leads to a rambling series of slightly slanting rooms lined with books not at all for sale. Among the couches and desks were a few people bent over books or papers. I spent a long time there, wondering if I should just stay in the bookshop and write. Could I even do it, camp for weeks in the bookshop and write? Leave off wandering long enough to write? After all, I was free enough to settle down. This was no family hegira, but my own. I was not responsible for gathering up the future to complete the journey. Time has speeded up, and all the generations are in me. Only I am heading west, but I am really heading west. I have been heading west since I was born. It seemed quite simple, when I understood it. Paris wouldn't do. This particular fork was out. It was part of an old trail, west of Austria to be sure, but not west enough.

Yet west enough was a direct route. The forty-ninth parallel, on which Paris sits, continues west to Montana, forming the border between Montana and Canada. All I had to do was follow it.

I left the bookshop. Just outside, at its entrance, there is a marker indicating kilometer zero. I took it to mean the point of departure for all measures of distance around the world. While I had noted it each time I'd entered or left the shop, this time it seemed a personal message, a point on the map serving as a mainspring to distance, the place from which all roads start. How extraordinary to have a chance to start at the beginning . . .

The College National Finals Rodeo Parade

Alittle past two in the afternoon, a few mothers with small children began setting up chairs and laying out blankets on the grass strip edging Main Street in front of the house in Bozeman I had rented for the summer. In Montana for the first time since finishing the book and returning from Europe, I wanted to see what it would be like to live in town. Besides, the house was cheap. By the end of the summer I expected to decide between living in town or out. That done, I would return to New York in the fall, get rid of my apartment and burn all possible bridges. That last was the least serious part of the move. One can always build a new bridge.

The women extracted sandwiches and cold drinks

from bags and coolers and passed them around to their children, settling in to be the first row for the parade that would begin at three. The College National Finals Rodeo is a major annual event in Bozeman, the grand finale to the year of collegiate rodeo, with top contenders from around the country. The parade kicks off three days of competition. I hadn't planned to go to the parade, but when I saw that it simply passed by my house, I really couldn't do anything else. To go to it I just stood at the front door.

A bevy of cowgirls on horses that almost seemed to dance up the street led off. The horses tossed their heads, arched their necks, twisted around to turn back, but were instantly turned forward again, controlled by the girls with deft movements of one hand on the reins. The other hand held a flag. Cowboys came next—slim, tall and straight in the saddle, looking rakish and not nearly so young as I know they are. Their horses were as high-prancing as the girls', and you could feel the spirit being held in check, as if both horses and riders were something wild.

These were followed by several floats depicting heroes of the West, among them an Indian maiden and a buffalo, or rather, someone dressed as a buffalo, and a number of farmers in overalls who were arranged upon a load of hay.

THE RODEO PARADE

Then, in order: the Belgrade Rural Fire Department truck; a brass band playing "It's a Grand Old Flag"; the parade marshall; the Bozeman Chamber of Commerce in a long white bus; an Indian in full headdress flanked by two cowboys (these three inexplicably on foot); a fraternal order wearing fezzes and making figure eights up the street on motor scooters. Suddenly, a cowboy loped back along the parade on a fast horse, as if he had to get an urgent message to someone, then turned without stopping and loped back the way he had come. Perhaps he had to let someone know the fezzes were in the wrong parade. Instead of turning downtown in Iowa City, they had simply headed west. But who could the cowboy tell? The marshall was ahead. He must have realized that and turned back. The unfazed fezzes continued making figure eights. Had they been making them for a thousand miles? All the way from Iowa City?

A brief interval was followed by a troop of high-stepping, arched-back drum majorettes twirling huge silver pom-poms; a two-horse drawn cart loaded with farmers and a large sign that said "National Champs"; five cowgirls carrying American flags, others carrying flags of each of the competing states and Canada; two country singers on a load of hay; the Cuervo and Lace Band on a long-bed truck; and Sheriff Johnny France.

133

His name had been in the national papers in connection with the case of two mountain men, father and son, who had kidnapped a local top biathlete, then killed her rescuer. France has written a book about it. Why not? If Watergate burglars and their ilk can write best-sellers, why shouldn't an authentic rootin', tootin' western sheriff?

After the sheriff, several women riding sidesaddle appeared. They wore maroon velvet, high-necked, nineteenth-century riding costumes. Two of them carried Montana flags. They all looked cool and unflustered, although the temperature in town was ninety-two, and the sidesaddle an amazingly uncomfortable way to ride a horse. I think women claimed their birthright when they began sitting astride, helping themselves to the easy balance men had always assumed. To ride sidesaddle now, by choice, is really a celebration of the enormous skill required to sit a horse this way and have the horse actually move.

Next in line was a small truck carrying actors from the Loft Theater, Bozeman's own; a troop of little girl gymnasts in glowing purple leotards doing cartwheels; more drum majorettes, also in purple outfits, waving purple-and-white pom-poms; a float with pretty girls wearing western, man-tailored pantsuits and cowboy hats and waving to the people along the route in that special way they are taught as candidates for the Miss College Rodeo title; a large John Deere tractor with two small children peering out the cab window at the small children standing along the curb, followed by a formation of tiny John Deere tractors like so many ducklings following their mother, then another large tractor with another, solitary, child at the window. Next, two cowgirls preceded a man on horseback carrying a flag that said "Last Chance Stampede, Helena"; two jesters on bicycles; a band playing and singing a country song that goes:

> When I die, I may not go to heaven
> I don't know if they let cowboys in
> If they don't, just let me go to Texas
> Texas is as close as I've been.

This was followed by a float advertising hot tubs; another fraternal order, these men mounted on glossy black horses with white bridles and reins; the Bitterroot Mountettes, a troop of women dressed in red-and-white outfits whose horses also had white bridles and reins; an assortment of fast-moving cowboys and Mexicans on horseback; a few buckboards and surreys; a very large man wearing a Hawaiian shirt in a convertible, announcing the opening of the Crystal Bar's rooftop beer garden; a rickshaw; two clowns on unicycles; a small herd of loping horses with smartly suited, cowboy-hatted women astride; a covered wagon; a truck carrying Smokey the Bear and his fire extinguisher (this in spite of the fact that Smokey had lost some cachet as forest policy veered toward allowing fires to destroy the pileup of combustible deadfall that accumulates when all fire is suppressed); more cowgirls; several women in long and glittering Arab robes, their faces covered by diaphanous veils the colors of their robes, the saddle blankets on their horses equally glittering; a truck pulling a wooden outhouse with a half-moon carved into the door; and two street cleaners.

The parade was over. The innocence of it was immense. It seemed to me the sort of parade you see in movies about small towns in 1917, the sort that doesn't happen anymore. But it did happen. It went right up Main Street, past my front door. I stood at the door a while longer and watched the mothers pack up their children and scatter in various directions. Within minutes ordinary traffic resumed its progress on the street. Then it was just a hot summer afternoon in Montana.

Dominique

The Lebanese woman stood in a small group of people not far from the buffet table. She was dark and slender, her black hair almost shoulder-length and well cut, her black leather suit with its broad, pleated shoulders and narrow skirt the kind of style I had been seeing the previous fall in Paris. She wore glasses with black rims that emphasized her dark eyes and perfect olive skin. She was the only woman in the room wearing eye shadow. Dominique. As the Lebanese correspondent for a French radio station broadcasting internationally and focusing on Third World countries, on the anguished places of the world, she approached the world without laughter.

Dominique's employer, Alain, the Paris-based editor-in-chief of the radio station, stood nearby. With his clear face and wavy light hair, the lack of humor in his eyes, he seemed perfectly cast to play the French journalist, as if he were an actor hired for the part. But the immediacy of his response toward everyone near him was pure journalist, the intellectual perched at the edge of action. The group gathered around Alain was larger than that surrounding Dominique, whose exoticism put her at a slight remove. She did not look like the Bozeman women, whose healthy, outdoorsy attractiveness clothed them in a kind of glowing similarity to one another.

Guests of the U.S. State Department, the two journalists were on a tour of America. San Francisco, Washington and New York were considered the important places, the places they would receive the real picture of America's power and achievement. But they were also scheduled to visit rural America. The U.S. State Department considers Bozeman, Montana, rural America. No doubt the residents of San Francisco, Washington and New York do as well. Perhaps it is, surrounded as it is by farmland and ranches, by wilderness that is the wildest in America outside of Alaska. Bozeman's population is about 35,000 when the university is in session, about 25,000 otherwise. Gallatin County, which includes Bozeman, has a population of 42,865. According to the 1984 census, the entire population of Montana's 145,392 square miles is 824,000, or 5.7 people per square mile. This is not many people, but it is 0.3 more people per square mile than lived here in 1980. In 1980, which was the last year for which I could find figures for the entire United States, in the *Montana Statistical Abstract of 1984*, the U.S. figures averaged 64.0 people per square mile. These are the sort of figures that might cause the State Department to think of Bozeman as rural. But in south-western Montana, it is the big city.

Dominique and Alain were being entertained in the home of an environmental activist and her husband, a soil scientist and university professor, by the Montana Council for International Visitors. The council, started a number of years earlier by the wife of a former minister who had become a professor of Family and Marital Relations, entertains a considerable number of visitors, most of them during the summer. The State Department would probably not send anyone to Montana in the winter unless it was one of their own being banished. Are Americans ever banished?

Most of the people present were from the academic community. The woman who owned the house had been president of the Montana Wilderness Association while I was writing my book and had been helpful to me. The book had been published a few months earlier. Now I had encountered her by chance. Thinking it might be interesting for the visiting journalists to meet another journalist, and vice versa, she invited me to the gathering, planned as a backyard barbecue to give the visitors a real picture of rural America.

I had accepted because I thought it important to begin meeting people in Bozeman. Nevertheless, I resented being invited, dreading, as I always have, actually attending any gathering that did not have to do with work. I prayed it would be canceled. The appointed day was the second of two of nonstop rain, the first rain in about six weeks. The Montana farmers were at least a crop short because of the dry summer, and the forests were burning because of it. Maybe this rain would be a reason to cancel, I thought, as I woke to it that morning. The party was merely moved indoors.

My hostess introduced me to Dominique. The other people around her receded into some background. I asked about life in Lebanon.

"It's hard," she said. "You live only for work. There is no cultural life in Beirut now, no recreation, no social life. You work and you go home. And you hope for the best."

I had a vision of her walking through the rubble of

silent streets in early evening, the streets of a great
and sorrowing city, a gray city where people hurried
along, eager to be off the streets, to be home, to lock
their doors, to prepare for their lonely evenings where
they passed the time waiting for war to end. There
seemed to be so many at once in Lebanon. I imagined
a sturdy old apartment house, something built by the
French, on some elegant residential street, and saw
her walking through the rooms of it, large rooms hardly used, on her way to the kitchen. I watched her prepare dinner in the kitchen, eat with the news on; the
day's papers before her, the day's revolutions, execu-
tions, losses and violations her companions over
dinner.

"Are you ever free of the sense of danger?" I asked.
"Or is the danger overplayed in our papers?"

"Everyone is in danger," she answered calmly, that
calmness that comes when danger is as much a fact of
life as hunger and the need to sleep so that one ac-
commodates to it in a way that allows for action when
action is necessary. What are the choices, after all?
You accommodate or you leave if you can or you die.
If you accommodate you may also die, but at least you
have a way to make it through the day until you do.

"Do you think of leaving?" I asked.

"Yes," she said, "sometimes. I have French citizenship as well as Lebanese. I think of going to Paris. Perhaps I will."

There was a moment of light in her eyes. Yes, of course, I thought. In Paris you could go to dinner with a friend, for a walk along the Seine . . .

Dinner was announced. The pot-luck buffet to which we had all contributed was arranged in the dining room of the handsome, very American house. I wanted to go on talking to Dominique, but she was engulfed by the movement of people into the dining room where we stood. Other people began to ask her questions about her views of America or to urge her into the line circling the table. Someone handed me a plate, and I found myself in the circle. People ahead of me put just a little of almost everything on their plates, as if the food were ceremonial, the buffet table an exercise in restraint. Well-brought-up as all of us in the room seem to have been, I suppose it is ingrained that we take less than we want of the things we most want. There always seems to be a delicacy with which people approach buffet tables in private homes, as if these particular rituals of restraint could keep civilization within the bounds of manageable danger. But when so much is spread before one, can I be alone in wishing to grab food with my hands, tear meat from the bone with my teeth, glut myself with the sweetest things? Naturally, my manners are perfect.

The Montanan, who hunts to put meat on his family's table, may in fact have provided himself with a more natural restraint, since his more primitive instincts have an outlet in the hunt. Perhaps we are most civilized when we live in a way that connects us most closely with our basic needs and instincts. Then we do not require perversions of our instincts in order to retain some form of instinct, yet fit into polite society. I define polite society as that in which, rather than killing one another, we sit down over a cup of tea, or perhaps the leg bone of an elk, discuss our differences, find them fascinating, and see how they feed one another.

Perhaps manners serve as an external device for heeding the inner message that we may not take all that we want, that we do not need all that we want, and that if we take it nonetheless, it is wasted. Some people do not care about what is wasted. They waste food and people and countries. Are people who are truly hungry for food really ever hungry for power? Could one who had ever been hungry for food become a tyrant? Would leadership based on an intimate personal knowledge of hunger have a chance at being humane? Once in New York I heard a physician say that, in the case of a catastrophic war, he would kill anyone trying to enter the place where he and his family had stock-piled food to see them through. It's true, he had never yet been hungry. But why is it easier on the human psyche to kill than to share?

I put a little food on my plate and wondered how I would get through the dinner, let alone the evening, in this place where everyone else knew one another and was at ease. I missed Dominique and wished we had not been separated, then found myself seated in a corner of the living room with a geneticist and her husband, a chemistry professor. They must have seen I didn't know what to do next and somehow gotten me to the corner with them. All the furniture had been arranged in a circle around the edges of the room. People sat in chairs and on the floor. Alain and Dominique ate together with several people in another corner. After dinner, as we wandered about the house, the hostess gathered us up, announcing it time for the main program of the evening.

The concept of an evening "program" startled me. It seemed like being on a national park vacation, attending the ranger talk that begins with the last evening light and ends under the stars and is always referred to as the evening program. I wondered if there would be a slide show about America.

We were the slide show. Each of us a full-color

projection on a three-dimensional screen of life in America. Beginning with the man on Dominique's right and going counterclockwise around the room, we introduced ourselves by name and profession, spoke a little about why we had come, asked questions of our guests and generally engaged in a discussion of some aspect of American life. Since Alain and Dominique were political journalists whose daily life was the world's struggle, and because most of the people in the room were politically active, the focus was largely on aspects of American political life.

There were about twenty of us. Several hours later, the room had revealed itself to be full of highly articulate professors, Democrats, antinuclear activists, environmentalists, retired colonels (two), women in the state legislature (also two, one a lawyer and representative, the other, older, a senator who had participated in Montana's constitutional convention that framed the constitution that has provided Montanans with so intimate and direct a participation in their government), one computer scientist, many writers of letters to the editor of the *Bozeman Chronicle*, a foreign affairs columnist for the major Montana papers (who was also one of the retired colonels, a Sovietologist), one housewife who presented her identity with the sense that she was the only housewife in the room, a city commissioner, and me. Several had lived for years outside the States. One couple had spent six years in Afghanistan, where they had helped start, and literally build, the University of Kabul before moving on to six years in Tanzania.

Rural America.

Seated near the end of the circle, so that most people identified themselves before it was my turn, I felt like a child in a room full of adults who considered the world and acted. My participation in the world seemed trivial; I knew so little; my credentials were so slight. That, combined with my shyness at having to introduce myself to an entire room full of strangers, made me sincerely hope for an earthquake. This was not farfetched. Bozeman sits on an earthquake zone. It may, though, have been somewhat irresponsible.

There was no earthquake. It was my turn. I said my name. That seemed hopeful to me. Perhaps I could go on. "I came here from New York to write a book about the mountains of southwestern Montana," I said. "And fell in love with the place. I felt it was mine. I felt a responsibility toward it. The Montanans I met seemed to believe it was possible to have an effect on the way things go. They seemed to believe they had a power to effect change."

"Not *believe*! " a woman interrupted. "We *do*!"

"I wanted to live in a place like that," I continued. "But when the book was finished I left. I was really looking for a place to live and wanted to make sure I meant Montana before I opted for it permanently. I returned to New York. I went to Austria because I had once lived there and been happy. I walked along alpine trails I had loved, realizing I craved Montana's wildness. I went to Paris, because it seems the only city equal to New York, and studied French. I treasure all that Paris is, but I walked through its soft, old beauty longing for the rawness, the exuberance of Montana. I wanted in on all that Montana is, so I came back."

My hostess mentioned my book, and the others asked me questions, allowing me to become a participant rather than an observer. Although I guess I already had. In my enthusiasm for Montana, my shyness had vanished. Montana had given me an identity. I had come home. For the first time, I felt that among people.

Alain introduced himself. Lucid, intelligent, fully present, deadly serious, he had taken in every word, every nuance of the place, of this gathering and this country. Nothing had escaped him. The Billings morning paper had carried a headline about a coup in Uganda. He had been amazed that a Montana paper, a regional paper, would have any interest whatsoever in a coup in Uganda, let alone make it a headline story.

"Now I understand," he said. "The meetings the State Department set up for us in the cities were to present us with the ideal view, the government view, of America. They did not prepare us for what we would find here, this spontaneity, this concerned intelligence. We expected provincials and gorgeous scenery."

"We *are* in the world," a man said.

"After its cities," Alain continued, nodding toward the man, "America has been an eye-opener."

Dominique closed the circle. She did not talk about America, but about that life in Lebanon and the situation in the Middle East that rule her life. Was America—this room—a forum for her views, a place she could spread her anguish out before her and see it, plainer than ever, in the reaction of her audience? Critical of the roles played by the U.S. and Israel, she was careful not to accuse, not to damn. Facts in hand, she spoke with even, well-considered words, aware above all that it was her own country tearing itself apart. The perfect journalist in her fairness, she observed, reported, did not judge.

Or did I think her fair only because her views agreed with mine? Had she, who must be somewhere partisan, tempered her passion for this particular listening audience? Was sympathy for the cause more important than some other version of the truth? Did that

matter? Bearing witness to the ravaging of her country, she retained some impartiality that allowed her to
continue seeing. Obligated to witness either in the
name of truth or some personal morality, she must
present what she sees to the world. The cost is in her
eyes that do not laugh. I felt she must want to scream
with the pain of it and the urgency of her own views.
Instead, she remains reasonable, fighting for her land
in the only way she can, with that careful, awful wisdom built of professional objectivity and personal
passion—a wisdom heroic and doomed. I watched her
and understood she would never go to Paris. I understood she could not leave her land.

It is, finally, the land that matters. All one can have
for oneself in Paris, all the grace and beauty and civilization of Paris, is nothing compared to one's own
land. Lebanon. Montana. The Wallowa Valley from
which Chief Joseph so sadly led his Nez Percé through
the Big Hole in the belief of freedom. Without the land
there is nothing. These people, in this room, knew
that.

Land. Wildness. Life itself. They are inseparable in
Montana. There is no other possibility here. Life, in
the control of raw and awesome nature as it is in few
other places in America, demands it. It is for this you
come; for this you stay; or because of it, you leave. It

is on the edge of wildness that the American spirit is most at home. For some of us, it takes a long time to realize there is a home. Yet, whenever it happens, when we arrive, we recognize it at once.

Crazy Mountains

They say the Crazy Mountains got their name when a woman whose husband and son were lost there went crazy looking for them. There are a few variations on that story, but they all add up to a woman going crazy. Crazy Mountains. Somewhere else in Montana, I came upon Crazy Woman Creek. There must be lots of crazy women here. Or maybe they're just more straightforward about it in Montana. Maybe a crazy woman is more noticeable in all this space, like some raging wind that sweeps across the prairies with nothing anywhere to stop it until it crashes up against the mountains. Here, tormented by the impasse, it knocks itself out or pours up the mountainsides to whirl about the peaks in all directions at once, or funnels into canyons or scours valleys. Maybe a woman out here is like the wind, coming and going as nature wills, carrying in her always the power to purify the air, rout extremes of cold and heat, gentle the earth ... or destroy it. It's no wonder women go crazy out here, living like the wind.

The Crazy Mountains, before their name, were formed as a volcanic dike system radiating out from a central core. A range of high, rocky, knife-edge mountains, they stand there, on the edge of the prairie, apart from all the rest, as if they had nothing to do with other mountains. From their heights you look west to all the mountains of Montana or east to the vast prairie, immense, silent, stretching like some golden sea to the edge of the world. That's all there is to earth—the Crazy Mountains where you stand, the western mountains and the prairie and, somewhere beyond the prairie's far side, the ocean. Some say other land lies on the far side of the prairie: rolling farmland and city land and ancient mountains and highways running all the way across to the ocean. But when you stand on top of the Crazies, you know you can see the whole of the earth, and you see there's no space on it for anything that doesn't equal the grandeur of the mountains and the prairie.

Sky, of course, excepted. The sky is grand enough. Angry over the mountains and ready to spew down storms that pull long, jagged streaks of lightning to the peaks and ridges; whimsical enough to engulf the peaks in gray clouds so thoroughly that, where the peaks once were, there is nothing but gray sky. One sees how arbitrary mountains are. They are here. They are not here. A stranger could drive through a valley on a cloudy day and never even know he'd been surrounded by mountains. What a flat, gray place, he might think.

Sky has the power to do as it will with the world, displaying it in sharp, brilliant light or sucking it back into itself so that it cannot be used anymore until the sky is ready. Over the prairies the sky is a sea sky, blue and darker blue, hung with sea clouds. In this sky there are no boundaries, except those formed by the universe. Odd, though, to think of that sky as ended by the confines of this universe. Odd that it is not possible to think of the universe as infinite. Before all those satellites began making photographs of the edges of the universe, there was a time one could. I even remember that time. Odd to think that, after all, everything is contained.

It was the Crazies that brought me to Montana in the first place. In 1982, a man I met at six in the morning in a cafe in Pinedale, Wyoming, told me he had just come from there. At six in the morning a few locals gather in every cafe in America. They come daily and, daily, the waitress sets down coffee before them without asking. If there are strangers present as well, the strangers have in common the fact that they are strangers. This constitutes an introduction.

I was on my way into the Wind River Range.

"I just came from the Crazy Mountains," the man said.

I had never heard of them. "Where are they?" I asked.

"Montana. My brother and I spent a week there. Beautiful. Those mountains are beautiful..." His voice trailed off. He looked as if he could see them. "Beautiful," he repeated.

"Are there grizzly bears?" I asked.

"No grizzlies. Just those mountains like a jewel."

In 1858 the Crow Chief Plenty Coups went into the Crazies on a vision quest. Except he wasn't a chief then but a ten-year-old boy. When he came out he told his people that the buffalo would disappear from the plains, that a race of white men was coming.

At that time the only white men in the region were a few scattered trappers living more or less like Indians, moving from place to place, leaving no permanent structures behind; nothing to mark their passing but a race of half-breed children and the opening of the

West. It was not until gold was discovered in 1863 that they came in droves and built towns. Two decades later the buffalo disappeared from the plains, the white man having managed to do in his brief time in the West what the Indians, on their own, had not done in their entire history.

After I heard about the Crazies, I knew I would come to Montana.

On that first winter trip, my guide at the Bridger Bowl ski area pointed them out from the top of the ski lift. We looked across Bridger Canyon and the broad Shields Valley and there they were, entirely beholdable, beginning to end, soaring sharp into a cloudless sky. Covered by snow as white as clouds, they hovered in sky as if they belonged more to heaven than to earth. They were not much more than thirty miles from where I stood. When I spread my arms wide, I could embrace the entire range.

It was one of the early trips the summer I was working on the book. Susanna and I hiked across the range from east to west. It had been raining for several days before we went in, but stopped as we started. After we came out, it rained again for days. We had been given clear days. There were no other people. There were high, sharp ridges and long scree slopes and gentle green parks; there were streams and flowers and crystal, dazzling nights. We climbed two thousand feet to a ten-thousand-foot pass and our first view of the prairie. It was no view, but a dream of the prairie.

Former Secretary of the Interior Watt wanted to sell the Crazies. He figured he could earn the government some money and get rid of property for which he had no personal use. Oh, he didn't actually care if they made wilderness out of all that rock and ice that constitutes the core of the Crazies, but that land surrounding it down at the bottom was something worth selling. Some of the ranchers down there probably think so too. Many of them have grazing leases on national forest land, for which they pay much below the market value, but have a tough time earning a living anyway. No small rancher has so far told me he wasn't losing money. How long do you hold on to the land under those conditions? They could make a goodly amount by selling this land to developers. You could fit a lot of subdivisions in there. Vacation homes. A good market. People put money into second homes.

They got rid of Watt and kept the Crazies. That was so logical a way to do things that one can hardly imagine it was done by the U.S. Government.

At first I just wanted to be in the Crazies. But now that I'd been in them, what I wanted was a peak. Crazy

Peak. Eleven thousand, two hundred and nine feet, according to the U.S. Geological Survey. The highest in the range. Chief Plenty Coups said he'd gone to the highest peak.

It took more than a year to get back in. Two summers later, in that summer that was so hot and dry, Bruce and I went there at the end of August. It was late in the day when we reached the trailhead. The sun was already low, lying on the sky in the long Montana dusk. We took the same trail Susanna and I had taken, but we would turn from it about two miles from the start, to reach Blue Lake at the foot of Crazy Peak.

Since that first summer, I had been watching Crazy Peak from the road as I drove past en route to other ranges, or back and forth from New York. It was always different—forbidding, beckoning, hard, easy, jagged, soft. It was everything a mountain should be. It was more; it was an obsession.

On the trail between the trees, the darkness came sooner than I thought it would. When it became apparent we would be caught by night, Bruce went ahead to find a campsite before complete dark. I welcomed his going ahead, welcomed the chance to walk here alone. I maintained a good pace at first, with the last vestiges of light, then picked my way among the stones that held some light, thinking how often in Montana I seemed to hike by night. The night wrapped me like a shawl, warm and soft. Nothing in the night could harm me. I was happy walking through it, although occasionally concerned I might miss the turnoff, which is not particularly well marked. There were no sounds. Nothing moved. I moved. Nothing else. Bruce must be very far ahead. He walks so quickly. It doesn't matter to him whether it's day or night. His feet are as sure either way. I wondered if I'd passed the turnoff. It seemed as if I'd been walking a long time. Two miles surely. Five perhaps. I can lie down, I thought, when I come to a meadow. Lie down and wait until morning. A small fire flared in a large black space to my right. Bruce. I crossed the clear, black space.

"I thought we should stop," he said.

We put up the tent and crawled in, hardly speaking. We had been fighting earlier in the day. I don't remember what the fight was about. I don't really remember what any of them were about. They happened all the time now. He had moved to Bozeman, and we no longer had anything in common except the mountains and our love.

In the morning we found the turnoff near the clearing, made our way across Big Timber Creek a few feet down the path, then continued down, the long descent like Alice's fall into Wonderland, revealing at its bottom Blue Lake, the mountains surrounding it, Crazy Peak to the south. Around the lake, and along the creek running down to it from Granite Lake, a few minutes' walk higher up, were many boulder-strewn, sandy sites to camp. Renewed by morning and the walk, the lingering unease between us submerged itself beneath the smell of morning and the hope of day. We made camp and climbed up beyond Granite Lake, about seven hundred feet to Druckmiller Lake, then a little above that for a view into Pear Lake, lying between us and Crazy Peak. Crazy Peak itself we saved for the next day, the day we would have an early start at it, the day we would devote fully to it. Scrambling over rocks on the way to Druckmiller Lake, we could clearly see the route up the southwest side of Crazy Peak, a long one over a broad, high, rubbly boulder field to the ridge, then a scramble over rock to the top.

Now that I stood before it, did I long for it still, or dread it? Was it possible that even toward this mountain I knew I wanted I was ambivalent? How was it possible to fear so much those things I wanted? Why could I not be so single-mindedly bent on my quest, as Plenty Coups had been, that the mountain was only incidental, a means to a dream? But the mountain *was* the quest . . . The mountain was not incidental. Watching it, I wondered if there was anything on earth of which I was not afraid. What flaw was it in me that led me to mountains, to a world where I must deal constantly with my fears, rather than one that might have been at least a little easier? Wouldn't it be nice if *something* wasn't a test? I try to imagine what it might be like, but come up empty every time. There is nothing else for me to do. Sometimes I avoid mountains, but those are the times they are most absolutely with me.

It was a gray dawn. Crazy Peak stood darker than the dawn, a harder gray against the gray sky. There were no sounds from the other campsites. We ate and started out, heading straight up the steep boulder slope on the lake's southwestern side. There was no beginning, no chance to get my muscles moving. It was not possible to ease onto the mountain. It was simply steep, the earth slippery, the rocks loose, the footing unstable. Bruce, who had climbed the mountain once before, slowed himself so I would not lose sight of him. He could have run up that slope.

I picked my way uneasily among the loose rocks. I hate loose rocks. The mixed earth and rock became less steep; became entirely rock, thousands of years of rock piled upon rock. Traversing the slope, we angled continually up. The sky darkened further. Rain would come. Lightning might come. The mountain was entirely open, exposed everywhere to lightning. On the ridge we would be the highest things around. The ridge was no longer far above us. Getting there would be easier than the first part of the climb, and climbing up the ridge to the peak easier yet.

"We have to turn back," Bruce said. "It's going to storm."

The mountain had been taken from me. It was not my fault. It was my fault. If I could have gone faster, we would have been there. But I couldn't go faster.

"You could have made it," I said.

"I might have been caught on the ridge or the peak. It's probably good luck I have to turn around."

Disappointment, failure, annoyance, relief . . . and renewed longing, because I had not yet got it. When I do, then what?

We walked straight down from where we were, now following our route of the day before from the lakes. That seemed to me a better way to go up. When I come again, it's the way I will start. I got off too shakily on that steep slope. From breakfast to a steep, loose slope. That's the wrong morning for me. Some people get up in the morning and go out and do a thing they've never done. I start slow. I need to work my way around the thing. I need to surround myself with it and enter it and then begin. This, of course, makes me totally unfit for expedition work, but then I would never have been physically strong enough for that anyway. My own mountains in my own time. That's not failure. It's a personal quirk. Why doesn't this make me feel any better?

I fumbled my way down after Bruce, seething. Once again I had proven myself inept, unskilled, slow, ponderous, when in my soul I would dance up mountains. Why is there so much distance between my body and my soul?

It was sprinkling as we reached camp. Within an hour the rain began in earnest. We huddled in the tent reading Hemingway. *The Snows of Kilimanjaro.* Harry lies on his cot, dying. No, Harry lies on his cot finally understanding that "now he would never write the things that he had saved to write until he knew enough to write them well. Well, he would not have to fail at trying to write them either. Maybe you could never write them, and that was why you put them off and delayed the starting."

It had been a long time since I had written anything. How did it happen that just this book was on this trip? Bruce had brought it, not I. I had not read Hemingway since college. Even in Paris I had not read Hemingway. Crazy Peak had given me time to read what I once thought was merely great writing, but what I now saw was truth. About writing. About climbing mountains. There wasn't much difference between the two. Sometimes you make it. Sometimes you don't.

The hard earth would not absorb the rain. The water pooled and ran in rivulets, now entering the tent. Bruce crawled out to scour out a shallow ditch around the tent. At once the ditch filled with water which itself poured out in wider rivulets. He crawled out again and deepened the trench. The rain continued.

We read *A Clean, Well-Lighted Place*. When I read that one in college, there had seemed to me to be a place where it was not clear which of the two waiters was speaking. It seemed necessary to me that it be clear. So I wrote to Hemingway and told him I didn't think it was clear. He wrote back and said, "It's perfectly clear to me." I showed the note to my English teacher, who asked if he could have it. I gave it to him. It never occurred to me it might one day be extraordinary to have a note from Hemingway. Not that I'm sorry I gave him the note. He's a poet and poets require talismans. I hope he still has it. But I hadn't read the story since then. Now, as I read it, I could not find the exchange that had been unclear to me. I guess Hemingway was right.

The rain lifted toward evening, although the sky

remained gray, as if the rain was not yet finished. Bruce was able to get a fire going (Bruce is always able to get a fire going), and we sat near it, eating dinner, when suddenly the whole top of Crazy Peak lit up fiery red, as if fire was inside radiating out, a brilliant red, rose light, some sacred luminescence. Aware, in the same instant, that it was not the mountain but the sun that made the light, we turned to see the sun behind us exactly at the moment it exploded out of the gray clouds, between two peaks, exploded in a million bursts of flame as if this was the end of the sun forever: one last, effervescent, squalling, bursting eruption of fire. Light now would be gone from the earth.

The sun was gone. The gray clouds folded in on it. The glow left Crazy Peak. We had been given a gift of Crazy Peak we would never have had on its summit. Anyone can climb a mountain, but miracles are rare. We did not speak. We understood that although we were losing one another, we had shared a miracle. We would not lose the bond of our souls, blessed by all the fire and glory of heaven and the earth.